THIS
THING
CALLED
CHRISTIANITY

JEFFERSON BETHKE

THIS THING CALLED CHRISTIANITY

A DANCE OF MYSTERY, TRUTH, GRACE, AND BEAUTY

NELSON
BOOKS
An Imprint of Thomas Nelson

Derived from material previously published in *It's Not What You Think: Why Christianity Is About So Much More Than Going to Heaven When You Die.*

Published in Nashville, Tennessee, by Nelson Books, an imprint of Thomas Nelson. Nelson Books and Thomas Nelson are registered trademarks of HarperCollins Christian Publishing, Inc.

Published in association with Yates & Yates, www.yates2.com.

Abridgement by Sam O'Neal.

Thomas Nelson titles may be purchased in bulk for educational, business, fund-raising, or sales promotional use. For information, please email SpecialMarkets@ ThomasNelson.com.

Scripture quotations are taken from the ESV® Bible (The Holy Bible, English Standard Version®). Copyright © 2001 by Crossway, a publishing ministry of Good News Publishers. Used by permission. All rights reserved.

ISBN 978-0-7852-3270-4 (HC)
ISBN 978-0-7852-3280-3 (eBook)

Printed in the United States of America

20 21 22 23 24 LSC 6 5 4 3 2 1

CONTENTS

INTRODUCTION
LIVING IN COLOR

If you went to a public middle school, you probably read a few classics for English class. I remember reading *To Kill a Mockingbird* and *Of Mice and Men*, among others. Hands down, though, my favorite novel was Lois Lowry's *The Giver* (which was also made into a movie).

If you're not familiar with that story, the basic premise is that an entire society is controlled by a group of elders who set up a system that strips all choices and emotions from humans' lives. Each person is forced to take an injection every morning that takes away these things.

Both the book and the movie communicate that every living person follows these rules, and seeing only black and white is the normal standard. There's no color, no life, no joy. But because of the injections, and because *everyone* takes them, they don't know that's not normal. They believe the world is black and white, and that it's devoid of colors and the blessings that come with them, and it's simply the way to live.

The main character, Jonas, starts to dream and have faint visions in color. He can't even describe what he thinks he saw, but when he stops taking his injections fully, *everything* begins to show up in color. It's so radically life-giving and beautiful, he doesn't have language for what he's seeing. It's too vibrant and hypnotizing. Nothing changed about the world he is living in, except now his eyes have become able to perceive what was always there. He quickly and clearly realizes the world isn't what he thought.

I believe our world has been stuck in black and white for centuries. For millennia. Culture after culture has pushed the same false narratives and empty promises on how to find purpose and meaning in our lives. *Success creates value. Winning brings happiness. Put yourself first.* Like the characters in *The Giver*, we don't realize that the picture of life we've been sold is incomplete. There's much more for us to find. Much more for us to be.

Finding those new colors, those new experiences, begins with finding Jesus. He is the source of true vibrancy in this world and in all of creation. And in an incredible act of generosity, he made the ultimate sacrifice to reach out and offer us something new—to spark a color revolution in our black-and-white world. That spark is called Christianity, which is nothing more and nothing less than people like you and me rejecting what the world is pushing and choosing to follow Jesus instead.

It's my goal in this book to show you that this thing called Christianity is a dance of mystery, truth, grace, and beauty. It's the antidote to everything dull and gray and hopeless. And it's ours not for the taking, but for the living.

INTRODUCTION

In my own study and journey with Jesus and the Scriptures, I've come to realize there are certain things about the first-century world that make Jesus and the Scriptures even more vibrant, beautiful, and compelling. When you understand his world, you begin to understand him all the better.

When we enter into the world of Jesus and take him for who he was, our lives begin to turn to color. Details we hadn't noticed before jump out at us. Stepping back into the first century gives us new eyes to see who he was, what he did, and why we are still talking about him today.

I hope through these pages you might begin to see the vibrancy of following Jesus in a whole new way. I'm not a pastor or theologian, and I don't have numerous degrees so people need to call me Doctor or Professor Bethke. But over the past several years I've fallen more in love with Jesus and the story of God and his church by gaining a better understanding of Jesus as first-century rabbi and letting him speak without my own interpretations and expectations getting in the way.

Every morning as I walk with Jesus, I ask him to open our eyes more and more each day. Because when we see Jesus clearly, then we can follow him. And that's the blessing of Christianity: we get to follow not some generic god but Jesus—the one who's always catching us off guard, creatively challenging us, pursuing us, and loving us.

INTRODUCTION

I've written these pages as someone who—like you—is on a journey to see Jesus more vibrant and alive, and for who he truly is more and more each day. Will you join me?

ONE

CREATION:
OUR PLACE IN
GOD'S STORY

It's been said that only a handful of basic story plots have been told throughout all of human history. There's "rags to riches," for example. There's comedy and tragedy. There's "hero versus monster" and romance. There are also more complex stories that use the same basic plots but just combine them or bounce back and forth between one and another.

It's a little humbling when you think about it. All the movies, all the books, all the plays on Broadway that have ever been written or produced can all be boiled down to the same few structures. The same few stories.

What about you? What story are you walking in? What's the plot? Who's the main character? What's the goal?

We all have answers to those questions whether or not we know them. To many, the plot is that life has no meaning, so you may as well enjoy it while you can. The main character is yourself. And the goal is to enjoy it—gain as much as possible, as easily as possible, with as little pain as possible. When I was in college, this was basically the story every one of my friends was living in.

Others live in a story that is driving toward Utopia. It's about continuing out of primitive religions, philosophies, and ideas, and making the world a better place one step at a time. Sadly, they don't realize that the most "advanced" full century we've ever lived in, the twentieth century, is also on record as the bloodiest. It seems enlightenment of ideas and philosophy aren't going to achieve a utopia.

So what's the true story? Which is the best story?

The truth is, what we know as Christianity is the greatest story ever told. And it all starts with the first three chapters of the very first book in the Bible: Genesis. It starts with the story of creation.

Genesis is a deeply beautiful, poetic, rhythmic, powerful book.

"In the beginning . . ."

Quite a start, right? Not "Let me tell you some facts, theories, and abstract truths," but "Let me tell you a *story*."

The first couple of chapters of Genesis are beautifully written. God makes order, beauty, and meaning out of chaos. Before God touched his finger to creation, the Scriptures say it was *tohu va bohu*, which literally means "void and empty." But God starts making stuff, starts bringing beauty.

If you've ever seen a painter at work in his studio or a carpenter making something beautiful out of the best cuts of wood there are, you can only imagine the scene when God creates *everything*.

And he just won't stop. Animals, stars, flowers, water, and land. And then, as the crowning act of

4

creation, he makes two image-bearers—male and female—and puts them into the garden to reflect, cultivate, and steward. He points them to the cultivated part of the garden where everything has been made right and tells them to make the rest of the world look like that.

What we need to understand is that those verses in Genesis are describing not only the creation of the world but also the creation of Christianity. It's the beginning of the story that leads us, purposefully and intentionally, to the Jewish carpenter named Jesus.

That's an important detail, by the way—that Jesus was a Jew and a rabbi. He probably had the Torah (first five books of the Bible) memorized, if not the entire Tanakh (Old Testament). The Old Testament is a lengthy, weaving, extensive collection of texts that seem to end without delivering what they all call for—a Messiah. A lot of us often skip from Genesis right to Matthew, leaving Israel's story in the dust. But there's a reason Jesus doesn't appear until Matthew 1: Jesus is the climax of the story, not the introduction.

Any reading of ancient Jewish thought would show the first two chapters of Genesis were critical to their worldview and to Jesus'. These were the chapters that concreted their very radical notion of monotheism, which was and still is a pillar of Jewish thought— one God over all creation, as opposed to many other societies at the time of ancient Israel who believed in regional gods of the sun, moon, and crops, among others.

Talk about a story! The joy, elation, and mystery there in the beginning. Purpose, love, marriage, intimacy—it's all there. And it's all wrapped up in this incredible idea called *shalom*.

SEARCHING FOR *SHALOM*

Shalom is the Hebrew word for "peace." For rhythm. For everything lining up exactly how it was meant to line up.

Shalom is happening in those moments when you are at the dinner table for hours with good friends, good food, and good wine.

Shalom is when you hear or see something and can't quite explain it, but you know it's calling and stirring something deep inside of you.

Shalom is a sunset, that sense of exhaustion yet satisfaction from a hard day's work, creating art that is bigger than itself.

Shalom is enemies being reconciled by love.

Shalom is when you are dancing to the rhythm of God's voice.

And in Genesis 1, *everything* was shalom. It was shouting out of every square inch of the creation and exploding in every molecule in God's good earth. It was a crashingly loud symphony coming through the best surround-sound system you've ever encountered, hitting you from all angles at the peak of intensity. Yet now it's a dying whisper, a fractured song, a broken melody, only brought back into the right key at the feet of Jesus.

Genesis 1 starts the story with an appeal to the fact that all human beings on earth have inherent worth and value because they were brought to life by God's very own breath. They are living creatures standing in the gap between the Creator and the rest of creation. All of creation God *spoke* into existence, but with us the Bible says we were *formed*.

God got particular and creative with us human creatures. He rolled up his sleeves when he made us and declared us to be *Imago Dei. Image of God.* He did not call us broken, sinner, or failure.[1] Which means our *primal* identity (the one most at the depths of who we are—in our very bones) is one given by the Creator himself. We are his. Do you believe that?

Even though a couple chapters later we discover the concept of sin in Genesis 3, we are still made in the image of God. It doesn't matter how broken that image is. Beauty is more primal than the curse, and we were children before we were runaways.[2]

Think about it: when a temple gets destroyed, and there is just rubble and remains on the ground, it is still a temple. A broken, cracked, messed-up temple, yes, but it's still a temple. Its primal identity doesn't change. It didn't magically turn into an apartment building or a deli when it crumbled. It's a broken temple that has no hope of fixing itself and is in need of massive restoration from the ground up—but it's still a temple.

According to this thing called Christianity, so it is with us. And that's the story we need to shout to the world. We don't have a hard time realizing how messed up we are. I know I'm broken. I know I'm deeply flawed. I know I'm not good enough. You don't need to shout those things out at me from the corner of the street with your sandwich board—*I already know them.*

But you tell me I have inherent worth and value based on who made me, not on what I do, and I think, *Really? Are you sure? But . . .*

That's subversive. In a culture that continually strips humans of dignity (homelessness, exploitation of the poor, objectification of women, abortion, euthanasia, and so forth), we have to return to *shalom.* We have to return to that special declaration God shouted over humans thousands of years ago in that wonderful garden—"So God created man in his *own* image."[3]

It doesn't matter how hard you scrub, in this life you can't get the image of God fully off of you.

Sometimes we have a habit of starting the biblical story in Genesis 3, with the introduction of sin in the world, rather than Genesis 1, which is where God starts the story. When you start the story in Genesis 3, however, personal sin is the biggest problem in the world. Sin management is the problem, and Jesus arrives simply to pay for your sin.[4]

In that way of thinking, the world doesn't matter. Creation doesn't matter. Only we matter because in Genesis 3 the story zooms in on the human condition. Now, is that true? Of course, but it's not *all* of the truth. When you start in Genesis 1, you start with shalom not just of humans but of all creation. When God created the world it had perfect peace. There was this beautiful dance that the trees, the animals, the water, the sun, the rhythms of life, and the living creatures Adam and Eve were all doing. No one missed a step.

But when sin came into the world, it fractured that dance, broke the rhythm, stopped the music. Creation stopped playing Beethoven's symphonies and started sounding more like sixth-grade me trying to learn my first note on the trombone. My mom didn't say, "Oh, that's so beautiful." She probably plugged her ears most of the time. It was *off.* And broken.

But when you start with the creation of all things as good, because that's exactly what God said about them (food, music, relationships, beauty, and all of heaven and earth being flooded with God's presence), then the answer instead isn't sin management but restoration of all things. God is putting his world back together, and to do that he's using the very people who broke it.

The level of reconciliation and restoration goes way deeper. God is recreating and remaking *everything* in the person and work of Jesus, and you can only get that when you get that he cares about all that in the first place (Genesis 1–2). Jesus declared a new world was bursting forth right here in the midst of the old one, and you can't get that unless you know the whole world needs restoring. Some people say this way of explaining and understanding the gospel message is taking sin lightly, but I'd argue the exact opposite. What makes sin bigger? Humans being affected by it, or the whole world (including humans) being affected by it? And when sin is that big, it makes what Jesus accomplished even bigger.

How we understand this comes back to how we see the Bible. If we don't see it as a narrative, we won't tell it as one. And if we don't believe God loves us for who we are even before we ask to be forgiven, then we won't really care to hear—let alone believe—his words.

HOW YOU SEE THE BIBLE SHAPES YOUR VIEW OF GOD

One of my favorite things my sweet wife, Alyssa, does began before we were married. Whenever I go on a trip, she writes me notes of encouragement, one for every day I'm gone. I hardly make it to the airport before opening *all of them* all at once.

I can't help myself. They bring me so much joy, life, and encouragement that I want to read them all in one sitting. (I was also that kid who begged my parents to let me open my presents two weeks before Christmas. Patience is obviously a virtue I hold innately.) I'm so antsy to read them all because I truly believe Alyssa loves me, is all for my joy, encourages me, and cares about me. If this weren't the case, I wouldn't be tempted to read them. We are more inclined to read someone's words when we believe those words are there because they care for us.

Do you really believe God loves you? Admittedly, the word *love* is a little fuzzy and overused in our culture. How about, do you believe God *likes* you? Delights in you? Knows you? Dances because of you? Because if you do, then I have a feeling that the motivation to pick up his grand narrative called the Bible won't be that big of a problem.

I've seen a lot of books and blogs on how to study or read the Bible. You can use all the techniques in the world, but if you think God is burdened by you, is aloof, or doesn't care about you, then you'll be predisposed to have a distorted lens through which you view him right from the beginning.

So what lens do you see the Bible through? A road

map to life? A sword? A collection of stories? Even though you probably don't think so, the answer to that question has cosmic implications. Your answer to that question ultimately gives you a very specific view of God and your role as someone under him.

For example, a common metaphor in the Christian world is that the Bible is the "sword of the Spirit." The writer of Ephesians (6:17) uses the imagery of a sword to explain God's Word has an edge to it; it's sharp and can create things. It can cut deep. It has power. It divides between soul and spirit, bone and marrow.

But if you see the Scriptures only as a "sword," it says something very specific about God. It projects that he is nothing more than a sergeant or captain who has commissioned us to fight in a war. And if God is a captain of an army, then that makes us soldiers. Of course, sword imagery is used in the Scriptures, but it's not the ultimate narrative. We don't see it in creation, the history of Israel, or the words of Jesus.

In fact, it's only used on a few occasions to convey a special aspect of the Christian life. So it's a subnarrative (meaning it's true and it's there), but it's an illustration used to serve a greater narrative. The word *soldier* isn't used nearly as often as *bride* or *child*. Elevating subnarratives to a primary status can distort the truth and create those groups of people you see wielding their "swords," quoting verses about "those" evil people, and creating an us-versus-them culture.

Another lens some people use is seeing the Bible as a moral compass listing precepts we should follow. The problem with that is a lot of parts of the Bible are things we certainly don't want to follow. There is murder, adultery, rape, incest, and a whole slew of terrible things. One way I heard a pastor say it that helps me is that the Bible is *descriptive*, not *prescriptive*. It's mainly about how God relates to a broken and rebellious human race, and in the midst of that narrative he gives some precepts and ways to live.

Still others view the Bible as nothing more than a road map for life. Of course, the Bible does contain some specific guidelines; Proverbs is nothing but advice given to the young as they embark on the world. But we have to admit the Bible is not the user-friendly manual we would choose. It doesn't tell us what college to attend, what person to marry, or what job to take. It does have razor-sharp focus on God's ultimate will being that we follow him, live humbly, seek justice, and be obedient.

When you view the Bible as your personal road map, you can't help but create a God who is a blend of Santa Claus and the Magic 8-Ball. He exists to satisfy your desires, answer your specific questions, and give you exact details about who he wants you to marry or what school he wants you to go to. This view of the

Bible places you as the center of the story. The world is revolving around you, and God is present as butler, not Lord.

There are plenty of examples of the Bible through different lenses. And while each view isn't completely wrong as a subnarrative, the problem comes when we give those distortions the ultimate importance rather than seeing them as simply pieces of the pie.

Remember, the Bible is sixty-six books and letters, written by almost forty different authors, and spanning more than thirty-five hundred years. Among the authors are kings, prophets, apostles, and shepherds. Imagine one letter written by President John F. Kennedy and another letter written by a fifth-century peasant. There would be enormous differences in the cultural, sociological, and philosophical frameworks they were operating in. And that's the beauty of the Scriptures. It's full of songs, histories, genealogies, and letters that have brought hope to millions down through the ages, written from many different perspectives, through different lenses, with different subnarratives.

With that in mind, the best way to view Scripture as a whole is as a *story*—a long story that is full of the bumps and bruises, twists and turns, plotlines, character development, climaxes, and conclusions every story should have. The narrative thread that ties these diverse texts together is God's rescue operation of this thing called humanity. The creation account, the Law, the Prophets, the songs, the Gospels, the Epistles, and the book of Revelation all tell the same story—how the Creator God (Jesus) brought about (and is still bringing about) new creations despite our rebellion, sin, and cosmic treason.

The Bible is about God—specifically about how God became King of the world. In Genesis, God created us so he could dwell with us and be our God. In the Old Testament, the mission of God *dwelling* with us is central.

- The Old Testament is all about what it will ultimately look like when God becomes King and restores this world.
- The Gospels are about what it looks like when God actually becomes King.
- The Epistles are about how to live in light of God being King.
- And Revelation is about the finality or conclusion where God is King and everything is in shalom as he intended in the first place.

And when we view the Scriptures as a story—more important, this specific story—we see our own roles *in* the story. We aren't at the center. We aren't on the main stage. The spotlight isn't on us. God created us to co-create with him. To co-labor in the task he commissioned to us. We aren't the story, but we are *in* the story!

THE GRAND NARRATIVE WITH GOD AT THE CENTER

Ultimately the Bible isn't about us, and that's good news.

Have you ever gone to a movie just to watch the extras? No one does that. Personally, I go to any movie Denzel Washington or Will Smith is in. I don't care what it's about. If one of them is in it, I see it.

But imagine watching one of Denzel's movies when, during a close-up of his face, you see something strange in the background. You squint because it's fuzzy and blurry. Soon, though, it becomes obvious it's an extra in the movie, flailing his arms, trying to distract from the scene. The extra wants the spotlight. That would be incredibly weird.

That doesn't ever happen because the movie is about Denzel's character (and that scene wouldn't make it past the final edit). When the extra plays his small role well, acting as a tool pointing moviegoers toward the main story (which means, if he does his job properly, he goes unnoticed), then the film flows perfectly.

That's us with God. We are in *his* story, his redemption and rescue operation. He is King. He is Lord. He is on the throne. And when we live our lives pointing to ourselves, we look just as stupid as an extra in the background flailing his arms during his three-second spot on camera.

We need to make sure we read the Bible as a *story*. After all, it's the greatest story ever told. It's the reason we all feel a whisper in our hearts every time we read a good story. It's a signpost pointing to the one all of us are in. A wonderful kingdom narrative with God at the center.

One of my favorite movies is *Amistad*. It's an incredibly gritty and raw look at slavery and Western imperialism. In one scene President John Quincy Adams is asked for advice regarding the court case defense. Adams says, "When I was an attorney, a long time ago . . . I realized, after much trial and error, that in the courtroom, *whoever tells the best story wins*."[5]

If we want our neighbors, our coworkers, and our family to think about Jesus differently, it's time we start telling a better story. *Whoever tells the best story wins.* As theologian N. T. Wright put it,

> Most Western churches have simply forgotten what the Gospel message is all about, and what the Bible, seen as a whole, is all about: that this is the story of how the Creator God launched his rescue operation for the whole of creation.

As a result, the great narrative the Bible offers has been shrunk, by generations of devout preachers and teachers, to the much smaller narrative of "me and God getting together," as though the whole thing—creation, Abraham, Moses, David, the early church, and not least the Gospel themselves—were simply a gigantic set of apparent authorities teaching about how unbelievers come to faith, how sinners get saved, and how people's lives get turned around. Of course, the Bible includes plenty about all that, but it includes within the much larger story of creation and cosmos, covenant God and covenant people—the single narrative that, according to all four gospels, reaches its climax with Jesus.[6]

What if we taught people to eat, drink, and breathe the story of the Scriptures? To see their own stories within the big story? To tell a better story than the world's narrative?

The fascinating thing is that there is some good science to show this is how God meant for us to learn truth, in story.

A recent study showed that the right-brain hemisphere—the one that controls creativity, story, and art—is wired and designed to receive and compute information before the left-brain hemisphere—the logical side that controls analysis and understanding. Meaning, we were created to take in the big picture and engage all senses through art and beauty before we go hash it all out.

Instead, letting our left brains take the lead, according to N. T. Wright, is the "cultural equivalent of schizophrenia. But these assumptions run deep in today's world, and they have radically conditioned the way we approach everything, including not least the Bible."[7]

No wonder Jesus didn't have his disciples sit down at desks, with him at the whiteboard.

Jesus' followers walked with him. And while they walked, he told stories—stories of sheep, lost coins, wedding banquets, different types of soil, a rich man and a poor man, two lost sons, someone coming knocking at midnight, and so on.

Jesus is the most creative, dynamic, and alluring teacher ever to walk this earth, and we relegate him to the mantel of our fireplace. No one's words explode with more power and draw out more wonder and awe than those of this first-century man from Nazareth, yet we prefer to give someone four spiritual laws or the Romans Road.[8]

It's about time we stop with the formulas and start with the truth and beauty of story.

We have the greatest story ever told, so let's start living in it and let's start telling it.

TWO

INCARNATION: GOD'S TENT IN OUR BACKYARD

Have you ever watched a suspenseful or mind-bending movie—some of my favorites include *Inception* and *The Sixth Sense*—that makes much more sense the second time around? You watch it again, and you see things that make lightbulbs go on that you didn't even come close to noticing the first time?

The book of Genesis is like that. The ancient Near Eastern world was very different from our own, and the authors wrote assuming their readers had the same cultural memory they did. Modern readers, such as you and me, have different cultural memories. We don't even come close to seeing all the metaphors and references in Genesis because we are so far removed from that culture.

If an ancient Near Eastern scribe had picked up Genesis 1–2, he would have recognized it as a *temple-building* text. Ancient Hebrews would have seen many markers in Genesis 1 and 2 that point to something we miss. Similar to texts of the time, it followed a structure that texts only followed when writing about a temple being built. All temple-building texts had two huge markers to distinguish themselves from other literature.

The first thing to recognize is that all temples, when they were completed, would have the image of that god placed in the temple on the last day as a sort of seal or marking that it was done. The second thing to recognize is that the builders would rest and celebrate the day after they had finished, and formally invite the god to take up residence. It was an ancient version of an inauguration ceremony. It'd be seen as a day of rest where you'd invite the god to flood the temple with his presence.

Sound familiar?

In Genesis 1–2, on the last day of creation, God the builder (1) places Adam and Eve in the garden as his image-bearers and (2) rests from his work, makes that day the Sabbath as a remembrance, and enters the garden himself. Hebrew and Israelite listeners and readers would have recognized those markers and said, "God is following temple-building patterns in the telling of the story." Genesis is all about a temple being built.

But the strange thing about this text that is completely unique and different from other ancient Near Eastern religions is that there's no building. No tabernacle. No brick and mortar. No temple.

Image-bearers always go in or on a temple. And they can't move. They are metal, wood, stone, etc. But in Genesis the images are flesh. A divine mix of spirit, flesh, love, and humanness. And Adam and Eve are placed in the garden, which is God saying loud and clear that from the beginning he wants to flood the earth with his presence. The whole world is his temple.

That's exactly what we see on day seven—God establishing his presence across the entire world. While other gods were regional and controlled only particular elements of nature such as the sun or sea or field, this God of Israel is God of *all* and God of *everywhere.* The ancient Near East saw gods a lot like how we see chief leaders of states.

It's totally fine and warranted to think the prime minister of Israel is prime minister in Israel, but not in China. And the president of the United States is exactly that: the president of only the fifty United States. But what happens if someone starts saying the president of the United States is actually president over every person and country in the world? That would upset a lot of people. It's not so subtly calling all the other leaders parodies or fake powers.

That's exactly what Scripture is claiming of God. He is God of everything, everywhere, all the time. And he's not a ruthless, fickle, borderline-schizophrenic god like the rest. Most ancient Near East gods constantly had to be appeased to keep the sun rising and the seas flowing and the crops growing. And if something was going wrong, you had to scramble quickly to find out what god you had upset.

But the true God over the whole world is a God of beauty. Of wonder. Of love. He creates a space where his children can flourish, and he cares about his creation and his image-bearers.

Today, the second most widely known creation story is the *Enuma Elish*, a Babylonian poem that was imprinted on seven tablets around the seventeenth century BC. Marduk, who would become the chief of all Babylonian gods, created humans to be the gods' minions. The making of humans is a side note to the rise of Marduk in this myth, yet in Genesis humanity is the climax of creation! We are God's image-bearers. We have a piece of him, are part of his likeness. He makes us co-creators and cultivators; then he sends us out into the world.

This was foundational to the Jewish story and deeply subversive after they had just come out of Egypt, which treated them as slaves without worth. This is also foundational to Christianity and our understanding of what it means to follow Jesus as Lord.

BRINGING HEAVEN DOWN TO EARTH

In Exodus, God tells us that he "will dwell among the people of Israel and will be their God."[1] Millennia later, John, the writer of Revelation, tells us he "heard a loud voice from the throne saying, 'Behold, the dwelling place of God is with man. He will dwell with them, and they will be his people, and God himself will be with them as their God.'"[2] This is a major theme throughout Scripture.[3]

So one of the overarching themes in Scripture—from the very beginning to the very end—isn't to "get people saved" but for God to *dwell* down here with his people. We are so concerned about going up to heaven, but God is concerned with bringing heaven down to earth. Revelation 22 even says the new heavens and new earth won't need a temple because God will be our dwelling place (think back to Genesis!). We are working so hard to get out of this place, while God is working hard to recreate and come down to this place.

Because dwelling is God's goal, he provided instructions for building a tabernacle (think *portable temple*) when he pulled the Israelites out of Egypt. God wanted to be in the midst of the Israelites. They were moving, so he would move with them.

Then later down the road, God gave Kings David and Solomon permission and instructions for building a permanent dwelling place for him.[4]

The temple Solomon built, with God's glory in the Holy of Holies, came to represent the Israelites' national and personal identities. It was the center of everything: Jerusalem literally was built up around it, and the people organized their lives according to its annual festivals. But Israel began to worship other gods. Maybe it was because they got tired of making frequent trips to Jerusalem, or maybe they just wanted perceived control over their own lives. Since the fall in Genesis 3, it was almost more natural to worship false gods rather than the real God.

The Israelites liked gods that were controllable, and the Creator God wasn't. They began to make a mockery of the temple system. They wanted to pursue other gods around them, when the true God Yahweh was right in their midst. There was one point where some even began following the god Molech, who called for child sacrifice.

As judgment, and maybe as a sign to wake them up, God sent the leaders of Jerusalem into exile in Babylon. They were enslaved to people who worshiped Marduk. The very presence of God was seen leaving the temple right before this judgment. And then the temple got destroyed.[5]

Can you imagine how this must have felt? Imagine the White House, the Pentagon, the Lincoln Memorial, the Washington Monument, and the Capitol were obliterated all at once. That's about as close as you can get to imagining what the Israelites felt when the temple complex was razed by the Babylonian emperor Nebuchadnezzar. They sing,

> By the waters of Babylon,
>> there we sat down and wept,
>> when we remembered Zion.

On the willows there
>we hung up our lyres.
For there our captors
>required of us songs,
and our tormentors, mirth, saying,
>"Sing us one of the songs of Zion!"[6]

They are undone.

A generation later, after Babylonia has been overthrown by Persia, some of the Jews are allowed to make their way back to Jerusalem and begin rebuilding the temple. But it's clear God isn't there anymore. The "shekinah glory," as it's called, never seems to return.

From this period until the last sentence of the Old Testament, the Israelites are left wondering when God will return to dwell with them. He promised he'd come back and be with his people. His very presence in their midst.

Can you imagine the hundreds of years of longing, aching, and praying for this to happen? With every year that passed, the expectation that God would do a new thing, a big thing, a monumental thing got larger and larger.

And then it happens. Just not the way they expected.

The gospel of John, while the Jewish people are still waiting for the glory of Yahweh to return to his temple, begins with the words

In the beginning . . .

Any faithful Jew would have immediately recognized the book's introduction as the same
introduction to Genesis—the book of beginnings and
creation, when God sealed the earth with his presence. John is invoking the Genesis language to get his
readers ready for a new story about another beginning, or a new beginning, in the same way you'd know
what I was invoking if I started a speech with, "I have
a dream, that one day . . . "

Skip down a few verses from that first verse and we
see one of our most famous Christmas verses. In the
beginning there is this "Word" being, John says. And
this Word being is somehow like God, with God, and
is God. You've probably quoted John 1:14 right before
sipping on hot chocolate and turning on Kenny G's
Christmas album; it's a classic advent verse:

"And the Word became flesh and dwelt among us."

But the Greek word translated as "dwelt" in that verse
is *eskenosen*, which can literally mean "to fix a tent."

John is saying loud and clear that Jesus himself is
pitching his tent (that is, his holy tabernacle) among
us. His body is now the place where heaven and earth
crash together. The temple system has reached its
fulfillment and was always a signpost pointing to the
great temple Jesus. The glory of God has returned to
his temple, and it looks like a Jewish rabbi in Judea.
How strange is that?

So John, in just a few verses, is purposely saying

things to draw strong echoes. Jesus is the new genesis, the beginning of a new creation; and God himself is pitching his tent with us—*to be with his people.*

What if we believed that?

Growing up I believed that Jesus was very far away. That he was standing up in heaven with his arms crossed waiting for me to get it right. Or even if he did show me grace, I imagined him rolling his eyes, saying, "Ugh, not the same mistake for the twenty thousandth time."

But John's words say otherwise. God really does want to dwell with me. He really wants to pitch his tent in my life. And when I continually fall, he says, "Hey, I'm in this for the long haul."

A GOD WHO IS VULNERABLE

Yesterday I did one of my favorite things: I got on the floor with our little girl, Kinsley, and basically made a fool of myself.

She can't walk yet, so we lay her on the floor with a few toys and watch her roll and tumble around the living room. I'll often hop down there with her and start rolling around on my stomach, laughing with her and just being on her level. I always talk to her in baby talk—you know, that language where you're saying nothing understandable and talking in a really high voice. I find it strange how normal that is, even though I clearly sound ridiculous.

When I jump down there with her, it's simply because I want to be with her. There's a special bond between a parent and a child, especially at that age, that isn't present between any other people.

Imagine I am going into a conference room for a business meeting, and upon entering I get down on the floor, rolling around and babbling. That would be weird, and the others would probably call the cops.

Baby talk is unique to my time with Kinsley, and in those moments I have no inhibitions. No holding back. Just simple childlike fun and love. And I love it. I'm not worrying about being efficient. I'm not worrying about saving face or making sure Kinsley knows our proper roles. No, it's just me rolling up my sleeves and entering into her world.

I think Jesus is like that. He's God on the ground with us—God jumping into our world and speaking on our level purely to connect with us.

In the Gospels, we see Jesus as the walking temple. God in flesh. The dwelling place of God now walking among us. But many of the Jews missed him. They wanted power more than they wanted love and justice and mercy.

In fact, they went so far as to kill him. They put God on the cross. *We* put God on the cross.

You'd think God would have reached his tolerance

limit and gotten rid of us all. Can you see all the pain and grief from God's point of view? Just think of a friend or sibling who's making poor decisions and choices, and how it literally hurts you. Now multiply that by billions, over thousands of years, and that's the pain we've caused God. He could have stayed high and lofty, but he knows love isn't possible without vulnerability.

So instead of blowing us off the planet after hundreds of years of rebellion, he resurrects himself from the grave and then sends his very Spirit to dwell in us! It doesn't get much more vulnerable than that. We can grieve the very Spirit of God because we are now his dwelling place, his temple.

God is forever taking one more step toward us, and every time he reveals himself, it's in a less guarded way. He wants to make himself known, and to do that he makes himself vulnerable.

The other gods seem high, mighty, and untouchable; they leave us to move first, to initiate, to appease them.

But this God, Jesus, says, "No. I'll go first. I'll lean in. I'll risk being hurt. I'll come down to you."

And he relentlessly pursues and chases. He shows that sooner or later, love will woo a human heart. Might we lean back into him?

God in the temple, God in Jesus, and now God in us. And the Scriptures keep going all the way to

Revelation 21, where it says we don't need a temple because God is our very dwelling place.

If you want a strange verse about what will happen at the end of time, read Isaiah 11:9: "For the earth shall be full of the knowledge of the LORD as the waters cover the sea."

The word *knowledge* used there is הֵעָ֫ד in the original Hebrew, which can mean "intimate." It's not knowledge of mathematics or science; it's knowledge of intimacy. If you're married, you *know* your spouse.

This is also the verse that says at the end of time, when everything is fully restored, God's weight, glory, and knowledge will cover the earth the same way the water covers the sea.

The verse sounds cute and poetic at first, but if you think about it, it sounds strange.

How does water cover the sea? We lived on a little lake near the mountains in Washington, and it's man-made, so they drain it every winter. When I looked outside while writing this, it was practically empty and all that was left was a huge dirt-laced cavern with a bunch of stumps.

When they took the water out of the lake, they took the lake too. Water doesn't just *cover* the sea; water *is* the sea. They are so interwoven that they are basically the same because sea is a type of water.

What God is saying is that when he finally reaches his goal and is fully dwelling with his people, in full intimacy, and sin, death, and all evil are gone, his glory and beauty will be so deeply covering the earth and our lives that they won't ever be able to be separated again. Similar to the water and the sea, his glory and the earth will be married fully as one, never to be separated again.

Is that the trajectory your life is on?

The cool part about the Bible is we can read the ending. And every time I do, I have to ask myself, is my life going that direction? Toward closer intimacy with God? Toward beauty? Toward him dwelling with me? Am I allowing him to take up residence in my life in all things? He's coming down and being vulnerable; am I reciprocating and dancing back with him in the music of eternity?

The incredible thing about this is once you step into it, it never ends. Once we start following Jesus, every day of our entire lives is about us getting closer and closer to our Creator. This isn't something you achieve or reach the finish line on.

Every day is a battle, and some days are better than others, but it's about resolving to put our moment-by-moment lives on that path. What can you do to put yourself on the right path? What little things can you do today to put you on the right trajectory? After all, you already know the ending.

THREE

INTIMACY: LIVING WITH GOD

In the garden of Eden, God created this beautiful and amazing world and put image-bearing humans (Adam and Eve) there to care for it, create within it, and reflect him to it. He gives them one law: don't eat fruit from the Tree of Knowledge of Good and Evil.

As its name suggests, when the couple eats of that tree, they will *know* the difference between good and evil. This implies that before they eat it, they *don't* know good from evil. So as humans in the world tasked with a job, how are they to know what to do? The only possible explanation is total dependency on God their Creator. The only way for them to avoid an evil they wouldn't recognize is to be leaning on God so completely that he tells them. So eating from the tree is actually saying no to dependency on and intimacy with God.

We don't need you; we don't want you; we can do this on our own.

In the West, this doesn't sound very offensive; our entire culture is built on autonomy and a pull-yourself-up-by-your-bootstraps mentality. But ultimately we have to admit there's something in us that tells us we weren't created to do this life thing alone, and that such independence leads to exhaustion.

NO MORE HIDING

In the garden, that command not to eat from the tree wasn't some arbitrary rule. I always thought it was the weirdest command, as if God were tempting us to sin. Like, God, if you didn't want us to eat from the tree, then why put it there?

But the tree wasn't a temptation to sin; it was an invitation to intimacy. Christianity is God giving humans the choice to live with him or without him. We can lean into him for what's right and wrong, since we don't truthfully know, or we can "eat the fruit" and have our own standards, ways, and paths. One choice leads to life, and the other leads to destruction.

And so in Genesis 3:4–5, Eve and Adam believe the words of a serpent, "You will not surely die. For God knows that when you eat of it your eyes will be opened, and you will be like God, knowing good and evil," and grab for the throne. Instantly they know good and evil. Something cracks. Something breaks. The fruit promised something it couldn't deliver, and the mirage falls away. The text says, "Then the eyes of both were opened, and they knew that they were naked." Exposed. Uncovered. Shamed. Guilty. Out in the open.

It goes on to say, "And they sewed fig leaves together and made themselves loincloths. And they heard the sound of the Lord God walking in the garden in the cool of the day, and the man and his wife hid themselves from the presence of the LORD God among the trees of the garden."[1] So the primal sin, the sin behind every sin, is saying, "I want to be like God. I want to know what's good and evil. I want to be fully autonomous. I want to sit on his throne."

Sin is less defined as smoking weed and stealing money from your boss and more defined simply as, *I know best.* And whenever we say we know what's right and wrong, we become our own judge and god, and that can play out in all sorts of behavior that isn't the best for ourselves or human flourishing.

Now, let me clarify that the issue isn't knowing right and wrong at all. The issue is *where* we find out right and wrong. Do we lean on God for what's right and wrong, or do we lean on ourselves? One creates life; one creates death.

But here's where I think the best part comes: That beginning part of the story shows the primal sin, but what's the primal response of God? What's God's first reaction after the humans throw a wrench into the entire system of creation? They did *exactly* what God told them not to do, and so God had the right to punish, to condemn, or to take man off the earth.

Instead, the Bible says God walks around the garden and asks two questions: "Where are you?" God is *God*, so I don't think he was playing a game of hide-and-seek with the first humans or looking for precise GPS coordinates. "Adam, what bush are you behind, bro? I can't find you." No, the question was a rhetorical one. It was a plea and beckoning with an ache in his heart. I can just imagine the sharp pain God must have felt in that betrayal moment. The beautiful world God had made and his relationship with the humans had been perfect, yet both were thrown out of whack in one quick moment.

God could have gotten angry. He could have left them to be in their own curse, but he does something fascinating. He goes looking for them.

Adam, where are you?

My son, my daughter, where have you gone?

You don't need to hide from me.

God's voice is always calling us *out* of hiding—that's how you know it's God's voice. If you're in a season struggling to identify God's voice, maybe ask which voice is calling you out of hiding and into intimacy.

It's only when we stop hiding that we can start healing. Every time I've experienced deep joy in my life, it was because I came out of hiding, asked for help, and admitted I couldn't keep up the act anymore.

But it goes on. God finds Adam who, probably with his face down, laments that he was afraid because he was naked.

God asks another explosive question: "Who told you that you were naked?"[2]

Who told you that you weren't good enough?

Who told you I didn't love you?

Who told you that you were a failure?
Because I sure didn't.

And God's questions haven't stopped since this very beginning. Throughout history up to this very moment, those questions echo throughout schools, offices, baseball fields, and modeling agencies. *Why are you hiding?*

I've heard his voice in moments when I've desperately needed it. From times when I made big mistakes in my personal life, to failure on the baseball field, to times I've messed up and let a friend down, God whispers, "You're good enough for me. You are loved. You are mine."

His voice always calls us *out* of hiding and *into* intimacy because that is God's goal. He makes it clear from Genesis to Revelation that he wants to *dwell* with his people. He desires intimacy, not hiding; transparency, not masks. To know God and be known by God is the dance of eternity.

But the Scripture narrative shows us throwing wrenches into his plan. It's us continuing to eat fruit of the Tree of Knowledge of Good and Evil while God relentlessly pursues us. God's goal is to dwell with his people, but it's a two-way street. For that to happen, we have to come out of hiding and take off the masks. We have to be vulnerable. We have to have our ears tuned to the heartbeat of God.

And rather than forcing us into submission, God

takes the long way and woos us back to him. He puts us on a trajectory that gets deeper and deeper into intimacy.

CHECK OUT THAT VIEW

From our backyard in Washington, Alyssa and I had this incredible view of Mount Rainier. We've hiked around the base of the mountain a few times, and it has one of the most breathtaking views I've ever seen.

Imagine we went hiking there but had never actually seen the mountain before. We had only heard about it from other folks, each one giving a little different description.

About a mile into the park we come to this big sign. It says "Mount Rainier," and it has a point on it. In our naiveté we think we've arrived. We say, "This is it!" We get out our phones and take selfies with the sign. We post them to let people know we saw Mount Rainier.

How weird would that be? We didn't actually reach Mount Rainier; the arrow was pointing us toward the right path.

What's fascinating is that's not too farfetched from what it's like with Jesus and us. The Old Testament is a sign pointing to the true reality.

Temple, sacrifice, Sabbath, and bread: they are pointing to something. They are pointing to the fulfillment of the promise to Abraham, but because God's children choose to worship signs instead of "walking humbly" with God, the first-century Jews missed Jesus, and we keep missing God.

Signs are needed on the journey. But once we reach our destination, it'd be absurd to continually return to the signs. And what's also interesting is signs don't give life. Just like with Mount Rainier, only the view of the mountain can amaze us and give us life.

It's at that moment of missing the signs so badly that the very creation God made to reflect and show his beauty killed him. Isn't that absurd? No other god was ever that vulnerable.

I struggle with a meek, mild, victory-through-sacrificial-love type of God. I'm too used to power being shown through force. We learn from childhood that true power shows no pain.

But this God stoops low. Comes close. Reaches out and touches us. This God is humble. Hungry. Sad. He made himself vulnerable to the very creation he had made!

The question is, why? Because *intimacy is his goal.* And you only get intimacy by coming close and risking hurt, pain, and rejection.

C. S. Lewis famously wrote,

To love at all is to be vulnerable. Love anything, and your heart will certainly be wrung and possibly be broken. If you want to make sure of keeping it intact, you must give your heart to no one, not even to an animal. Wrap it carefully round with hobbies and little luxuries; avoid all entanglements; lock it up safe in the casket or coffin of your selfishness. But in that casket—safe, dark, motionless, airless—it will change. It will not be broken; it will become unbreakable, impenetrable, irredeemable.[3]

Throughout the Scriptures you see this God, risking himself to get his goal. From the call and ache of the garden all the way to Jesus' crucifixion.

When God sees that Cain murdered his brother, he asks, "What have you done?"

In Egypt, he considers a crime against his Hebrew people a crime against him. When Israel is disobedient to the point of destruction, to the cries of the prophets, God wonders when his children will get that he just wants them, not their halfhearted sacrifice. Their full selves. Their hearts. Them without the masks.

And Jesus echoes this ache of God by saying how he longed to gather his people as a hen gathers her chicks, but the people were not willing. Even so, it says he weeps over the city since they do not know the things that make for peace.

It's as if God was longing for *echad*, but his children weren't ready.

Echad is first mentioned in the garden. It says a man and a woman, when they join together, become *echad*, or "one." But that word *echad* is more explosive with meaning than just one flesh. It can literally mean to fuse together at the deepest part of our beings. Two becoming one, completely glued together, completely meshing.

I still remember one of the hardest conversations I have had with Alyssa. We were sitting in the car after a wonderful date night. We knew marriage was a possibility on the horizon, and I felt like I finally had to share things in my past that would affect her if we got married.

I was incredibly nervous, as well as terrified of rejection or hurt, but I realized that if intimacy were to grow, I had to get vulnerable. For marriage to be what it truly is—two people becoming one in mind, body, soul, and spirit—I had to be honest.

I remember sharing with her many things, but specifically some details of my sexual past. My teenage years were littered with me almost worshiping sexual fulfillment in pornography, partying, and girls. And I say worship, because that was where I got my worth, value, and purpose as well as what I most lived for (which is what the definition of worship is).

I had to apologize and ask forgiveness from Alyssa for things I had done before I even knew her because of *echad*—one form of complete and utter intimacy.

Because of that beauty, mystery, and power, God created it to function best in a man and a woman coming together for life and constantly *echading* or fusing together.

I needed forgiveness because I had betrayed *echad*. I had betrayed oneness. I had betrayed intimacy. And if I wasn't honest about it, it'd be a little part of my life or heart that Alyssa didn't know—thus blocking *echad*.

But something really peculiar happened in that moment. With the grace and forgiveness of Jesus, Alyssa forgave me. She heard all that I was and am, and still wanted to walk this journey with me. I still remember the tenderness in her voice as she spoke truth and forgiveness over me.

In that moment I was exposed and *known*, and yet because of Alyssa's grace, I was at the same time *loved*. And that is where intimacy is found—to be fully loved and to be fully known.

To be fully loved but not fully known will always allow us to buy the lie that "if they only knew the real me, they wouldn't want me anymore." And to be fully known but not fully loved feels sharp, painful, at a level of rejection that hurts so bad.

But to be fully known and at the same time fully loved, now that is intimacy.

FOUR

IDENTITY: UNDERSTANDING WHO YOU ARE

One of my favorite movies of all time is *Back to the Future*. I got the special edition trilogy DVD set when it was released on Christmas back in high school, I dressed up as Marty McFly one year for Halloween, and I enjoy saying "Great Scott!" any chance I get.

When anyone is wearing a puffy vest in the winter, I immediately ask, "Ay, kid, what's with the life preserver?" If they laugh and get the joke, I know we can be immediate friends. If they stare at me awkwardly, I know they are one of those poor souls who has never seen the movie.

One of the premises of the movie (and any time-travel movie for that matter) is when Marty goes back (or forward) in time, he stands out. He knows things, has seen things, and acts differently because he is from the future. In the first film, there are some scenes where he is thought of as weird for making really peculiar decisions because his peers don't understand where he's coming from.

I like to view Jesus followers in the same way. When we walk in line with this thing called Christianity, we stand out.

If you jump back two thousand years to when Jesus was walking the earth, a majority of the Jewish people believed in the resurrection. They believed at the end of time, when God set the world right, the righteous would be resurrected and vindicated. The twist is that Jesus did that in the *middle* of history, not at the end. God did for Jesus in the present what Jewish people thought he'd do for all at the end.

In the resurrection, Jesus became a person of the future. He threw a lasso around God's future promise, and he ripped it into the here and now. He brought in a new world, a new way of living, a body that doesn't decay, one that is full of beauty and glory. And then he told his disciples to go and implement that. Go work it out. Bring that promised future into the present. And that's what Christianity is supposed to be.

Identity, or the idea of defining who we are, is primarily about living as if the future restoration has happened right now. It's imagining what will be true when heaven and earth are fully reunited and grabbing on to that now. Jesus has already resurrected, and that resurrection power is in every one of us who trusts Jesus.

God calls us to live as our future selves right here in the present, and by his Spirit he gives us the power to do so. One of my favorite quotes is, "Easter was when Hope in person surprised the whole world by coming forward from the future into the present."[1] Some of you might think this is a little funky, but we see it all the time in our world. For example, we call someone president-elect after the election but before the inauguration. And he is allowed to put into practice in the now what will be true very soon in the future. He gets secret service detail and millions in funding from Congress before he takes office.

We also do it with kings. David, in the Old Testament, was anointed king long before he sat on the throne. But he was called, the minute he was anointed, to live as God's anointed one. He was called to pull the future into the present.

The question is, when does this start? Or to put it another way: Where's the DeLorean?

For Jesus, it's his resurrection; but for us, we step into the future when we are baptized.

THE BEAUTY OF BAPTISM

Baptism is a deeply mysterious and beautiful act in which we step into our future and declare we are identifying with Jesus in his death and resurrection. It's stepping into what God says is true about us.

Jesus' own baptism invoked deeply held stories of the exodus—the Israelites leaving Egypt, trusting God, and stepping through into their future, the promised land. The exodus story was arguably the most valued narrative of the entire Jewish faith. It is still celebrated as the time God rescued his people out of slavery. Israel itself went through its own sort of baptism coming through the Red Sea. When evil was left at the bottom of the water, the Israelites were referred to as God's firstborn or God's son. After Jesus' baptism, he headed into the wilderness as if he was Israel personified.

Of course Jesus didn't need to be baptized. He was clean. He was God. He was beautiful. But instead of standing back and pointing fingers, he jumps right in and identifies with his people. He steps into the waters as a way of saying, *I'm for you, and with you.*

And something crazy happens. He hears his Father's voice thunder down from heaven, declaring, "You are my beloved Son; with you I am well pleased."[2] The Father speaks Jesus' identity over him.

Remember, this was the *beginning* of Jesus' ministry. He had not done anything yet. No healings. No preaching. No cross. No resurrection. This voice came *first.*

A lot of times we do a bunch of stuff and then hope the voice of approval and love will come after that. This basically describes my whole life. Trying to have a good year in baseball so my friends and coaches would tell me I was awesome. Getting good grades so I could be affirmed. Being as religious as I could so others would think I was a good person.

We hope to hear we are children of God at the end of the road, but God thunders it in the beginning. We hop on the treadmill of life, hoping that when the timer runs out we will hear, "Well done, my child." When, in fact, God declares that over us *before* we get on the treadmill. It puts us on a new journey entirely.

Why do you do what you do? Why do you get up? Why do you work? Why do you play sports? Why do you try so hard in school? Is it because you're trying to get the Father to tell you he loves you, or are you giving life all your energy because you know he *already* loves you? When you live in the latter, you live more freely because you know failure isn't a deal breaker but an opportunity to learn and get back up again.

So back to Matthew's version of Jesus' baptism. God says Jesus is a son, a child. He is the *Beloved*. The word *beloved* implies a special affection or place in God's heart for Jesus. But the beautiful thing is when we trust in Jesus, we are wrapped up into him. So when we are baptized, we are stepping into the future. The future of belovedness that is true right now. You are God's beloved.

And God doesn't sprinkle his love; he drenches us in it. *My child, my child, my child. I am well pleased.*

Can you hear the Father's heart? Have you ever listened to his voice?

The crazy thing about water is it's able to get through every crack it encounters. It moves, changes shape, floods, and permeates every little crevice.

That's how God loves. Where there is even the slightest hint of surrender and release, the slightest crack in our autonomy, God's healing love floods in.

I like how Jonathan Martin puts it in his book *Prototype*: the scandalous thing about Jesus and his baptism is that when God declared he was well pleased in him and that he was the Beloved, Jesus *believed him.* He goes on to say, "And unlike every other person in human history . . . he never forgot."[3]

After we realize we are beloved, there sometimes comes a season when God wants to brand that into us. To let it sink in. Become real. If Jesus went straight from baptism to ministry, preaching, healing, and the cross, God's voice might get drowned out. Noise is a powerful thing, and the noise of life can sometimes mute God's soft whisper of belovedness. But then something crazy happens. Jesus' hair is still wet as he starts walking toward the wilderness. He goes to the unknown. The place of chaos. The place where Israel wandered for years and years and years. Where they failed. Where people died.

A place of silence. That's where the future gets ripped into the present.

On our two-year anniversary, Alyssa gave me a sweet, thoughtful, long card of love and encouragement. One thing stood out to me, though: she started speaking the future into the present me. She encouraged me by calling me steady, gracious, loving, and humble.

What's funny is that I don't think those are things I actually am. I try to be those things but fail frequently.

Anyone who's been encouraged by a loved one, a parent, or a close friend knows nothing infuses you more with strength, confidence, and peace than a person filling you up with encouragement like that.

When I read Alyssa's letter, I felt like a superhero. Now, am I those things? Maybe feebly sometimes, but certainly not always. What's important, though, is that Alyssa believes I am and can be. And there's something deeply mysterious about it all, but when she says those things about me and constantly reminds me and encourages me, guess what? I start to become those things! It's as if she's speaking the future to me in the present.

If a loved one can speak such life, or such future, into us, then how much more power is there when the very Creator of the universe does it? He speaks over us, he delights in us, and when we are in Jesus, he tells us our futures are true right now in this very moment.

If you really believe that, and if you really listen to that, nothing can hurt or stop you. I know it might look good on paper right now, but do you really believe that? Have you heard that voice? Do you put your ear toward Jesus and listen?

WHAT VOICES DO YOU LISTEN TO?

The security that we have in Jesus doesn't do much for us unless we trust it and listen to it. Similar to a life vest, it only becomes helpful once we wear it.

One way to really rest in our identity is to make sure we are listening to the right voices. Identity is primarily a battle of voices. What do you listen to? Or who do you listen to?

In the first century, Jewish communities would hold a *kezazah* (literally, "to cut off") ceremony if someone from the village married a Gentile woman or sold family land to Gentiles. If the leaders of the community saw the offending man try to enter the village, they would grab him, bring him to the center of the village, and break a pot (usually filled with grain) at his feet. The pot was a sign of the community's relationship with the son. It was broken and could never be restored. He was cut off from the community, no longer welcome there.

This tradition seems to be lurking in the shadows of Luke 15 and the parable of the prodigal son.

The younger son asks for his inheritance, and then only a few verses later we are told he's already squandered everything and must hire himself out to feed pigs. Scripture even says the pigs were eating better than he was! Not only do we sense the deep despair and low point, but the cultural shadow looming in this text is he lost his inheritance, and the place he lost it was with someone who owned pigs, namely a Gentile.[4]

As he approaches his father's tent in disgrace, an incredibly scandalous thing happens: the father *runs* to his son. Running was a deeply shameful thing for Middle Eastern men to do. That was for children, not for a dignified and proper patriarch. But the father was willing to bear that shame because he wanted to be the first person to greet his son. The father would have known the kezazah ceremony was warranted, so he ran to make sure his was the first voice over his son. He speaks truth:

"You're loved."

"You're known."

"I don't see your mess; I just see you."

What's the first voice over you? It's the voice of a Father running to you with open arms. It's a Father declaring that you are his child. (Notice, in that story the father immediately went into declarations that explicitly meant sonship—the robe, the ring, and the party.) The son didn't have to do anything to earn passage back into the family. He was lavished with grace, love, and mercy. And the robe and the ring even meant he got more inheritance! All the father had was now his again, simply because love made a way. God's voice creates inheritance, speaks love, and gifts mercy.

When voices come, which do you listen to? Shame? Guilt? Disgust?

Or do you listen to the first voice over you? It's called the *first voice* because it was there back in the garden before anything else started to compete with it. The voice that's been calling over you since the beginning. The voice that started in the garden and has echoed down to us now: "My son. My daughter. My child. My beloved."

I'm not telling you to trust the first voice that comes in your head. I'm saying that God's voice was before anyone else's voice, and that's the one we should be listening to. I know how hard it is to recognize God; I've almost trained myself to listen to the voices of shame and failure. I recognize the enemy's voice more than God's because for so long I listened to his instead of to Jesus.

When we are in the Scriptures—the Gospels specifically—on a daily basis, then Jesus' voice is clearer. These ancient texts, narratives, and songs have a way of waking my heart to the Holy Spirit. How awesome is that?

WHO YOU KNOW IS BETTER THAN WHAT YOU DO

In elementary school I was quite the problem child. I was bored. And when a little boy is bored, he usually gets into trouble.

Routinely I'd do things such as turn off the lights in the bathroom when boys were in it, shoot spit wads at other kids, and other dumb stuff ten-year-olds do.

A lot of my mischief happened during recess. I'd throw something at a kid, kick a ball at them, or say something to egg them on. Now, I am not the tallest or biggest guy, and elementary school was no exception. I was arguably the smallest kid in every class until high school. So when I would do stuff like this, I knew I had to be able to outrun the kids because I sure couldn't outfight them if they came after me.

Eventually I learned I didn't have to run forever. I just had to run fast enough to get my friend Big Mike. His name is pretty self-explanatory, and I'm sure my imagination is fooling me, but I remember a five o'clock shadow, flannels, and axes at age nine.

I was one of his closest friends, and the beauty of that was, if I did something stupid and a kid started to chase me on the playground, I just had to run to the safety of Big Mike's shadow. If I got there, the other kid would stop dead in his tracks and just give a look. I was safe, and they wouldn't touch me since I was next to Mike.

When those kids wanted to beat me up, they didn't stop because of anything I did. They stopped because of who I was with. They stopped because they weren't scared of me but they were scared of him.

That's a little bit of what it means for Jesus' identity

to be our identity. The phrase "in him" pops up in the New Testament more than one hundred times (by the way, if something is pushing triple digits, it's probably an important theme). What's true of Jesus is true of us, and when we trust him, he is our advocate. Anytime Satan whispers lies to you, you can just point to the person next to you. Jesus is blameless, which means we are too. He's righteous, which means we are too. He's got perfect access to the Father, which means we do too.

Too many times we try to defend ourselves when false voices start coming into our heads. But in defending ourselves we feel the ground slip beneath us. Instead, we should run to the one who is our identity, Jesus himself. Demons aren't scared of us, but they are scared of him, and he's our advocate.

We are also children of the King, and that makes us dangerous. An attack on us is an attack on the royal family. You don't mess with the prince because you're scared of the king.

Have you ever seen those movies that involve a king? There's usually at least one scene where they want to show the opulence of the throne room so the double doors whoosh open and with a super-wide-angle lens we start moving down the red carpet toward the throne. Most often, though, right next to the king we see his guards. Usually in some type of armor, with a dead-serious look on their faces.

They look stiff, frozen, and cold. They are employees of the king, and they have a job to do. If they mess up, more likely than not they get fired. How weird would it look if the guards just started dancing around the throne room, running in circles, playing with their weapons, and jumping up and down with glee?

But that scene wouldn't seem out of place if they were children. There's this freedom afforded to children that they can have a playfulness about them. It would only go to show the tenderness of the king's heart if you entered the throne room to see kids running around the throne, jumping up and down, and having fun with Daddy.

The kids have different privileges than the guards. But sadly, a lot of us pretend we are the guards. With God we are stiff, cold, serious, and afraid of getting fired. We are walking on eggshells. But a kid doesn't get fired. A kid can have the joy and freedom that only a kid can have.

Which picture more describes your relationship with God?

Are you terrified you are going to mess up all the time, or are you playfully running around God's throne knowing your Dad is the King of the universe? God didn't come to make guards; he came to find his children. Jesus didn't hear, "This is my employee" at his baptism; he heard, "This is my beloved Son, with whom I am well pleased."[5]

When you look at your life, what do you see? Are you burned out? Are you tired? Exhausted?

There are voices creating that exhaustion. Voices creating that hurt. But there's another voice, a greater voice, a primal voice that is declaring over you right now that you are loved. You are known. You can run to the Father and know he will catch you.

FIVE

SABBATH: THE BLESSING OF REST

Devotional author Lettie Cowman wrote about a time when she visited Africa. She was hoping to make the trip fairly quick, so she found particular guides she thought could help her make it as efficient as possible. During the first day of the trip, she was pleasantly surprised with how much progress they had made. On the morning of the second day, however, all the guides refused to move and stayed seated. Since she had hired and was paying these guides, she was frustrated and asked the leader why no one was continuing the trek—especially at the pace that was seen the day before. He responded by telling her they had traveled too far too quickly, and now they were "waiting for their souls to catch up to their bodies."[1]

When was the last time you rested and let your soul catch up? When I look back and try to answer that question, I'm afraid my soul, my well-being, might be not just days but years behind me.

The word *sabbath* literally means "to cease."

When's the last time you ceased? Unfortunately many of us can't answer that question because we don't know.

A lot of us would respond, "But there's too much to do! We don't have time to rest!"

If someone approached you and offered the incredible gift of an extra day every week—meaning instead of seven days, every week is now eight days long—would you take it? What if the only caveat was you could only have the day if you didn't work. You had to play, enjoy family, eat a good meal, do something that fills and stirs your soul. Then would you take it?[2]

We already have an extra day a week for that *exact* thing. God already built a day of rest into the rhythm of the universe, and it's a vital ingredient in this thing called Christianity.

SPIRIT OF SABBATH

I love big cities, history, and culture, so naturally Jerusalem is one of my favorite cities in the world. (New York City might be a close second.) Even though I've only been there once, it was for a good chunk of time, and it wasn't the usual Western Christian trip. We saw the "Jesus sites," but that was only a day or two out of our journey.

We were staying with a mentor friend and family member whose family splits time between the States and Jerusalem. They have an apartment just a mile or so from the Old City, so we were in the middle of everything.

One of my favorite parts about being there was the celebration of Shabbat. On Friday night at dusk, a huge horn blows in the western part of the city that signals to everyone it is Shabbat. Within a few moments, instead of hustling and bustling, all you hear is silence. Besides the occasional car, practically no one is walking, driving, or outside at all, for that matter. It's kind of eerie.

The family we were staying with had a beautiful rhythm on that night, and the entire family seemed to partake in the preparations. They'd light a candle as a sign or put a stake of remembrance in the ground. That candle would burn the entire twenty-four hours. Then to begin Shabbat there would be a reminder that this day was about ceasing, about resting, about enjoying. The parents would pray and bless the five kids, and then we would all, usually emphatically led by the kids, bang on the table and clap our hands and sing a Shabbat song before dinner. Then we'd open a bottle of wine and have an amazing meal.

There was something sacred about it. Something mysterious. Something beautiful. No electronics. No looking down at our phones or scarfing down food so we could go play video games or watch TV.

Now that is a Sabbath. When I was at their table, I realized this was what life was about: Relationships. Food. Deep conversations. Intimacy.

We were there for a few Fridays, so we got to enter into their rhythms more than once. The next week was one of those rare moments (I can only recall a handful) when I felt the tangible presence of God and a weight of love and grace I had never before experienced.

It was about an hour before Shabbat dinner, and the family had decided to have a time of worship with another family who lived above them. We sang, we prayed, we celebrated, and we remembered what God has done for us.

At that time Alyssa was about four months pregnant with Kinsley, and because of her being pregnant and the fact we were their guests, they asked us to put our two chairs in the middle of the circle so they could encourage and pray for us. They surrounded us and laid their hands on us, which immediately added another level of intimacy and touch. I remember feeling so humbled in that moment.

They began thanking God for us, thanking God for this new life he was giving us, and thanking God for our future as a family. Even the kids prayed for us. To have eight different kids ranging from five years old to teenagers lay their hands on us and pray for us was humbling beyond belief.

In that moment I felt fully human. Fully loved. Fully known. Heaven had crashed into earth and set up an altar. Time seemed to pause, and love flooded in. The emotions still feel fresh just thinking about that night right now.

That's a Sabbath I'll never forget.

Rabbi Abraham Heschel makes the point that what temple is to space, Sabbath is to time.[3] Meaning, a temple is a sacred space. A place where heaven and earth meet in a physical place.

Sabbath is when heaven and earth meet in time—in a moment. Especially in our Western, work-addicted society, we need to set aside sacred time that resists the addiction to work, technology, and consumerism. Time isn't sacred to us. It's a commodity, and we all treat it as such. It almost shocks me to realize that for the larger part of history, people didn't have clocks or endlessly plan the day out to every minute—eat at this time, hold work meetings during this time, take the kids to soccer practice at this time. We are slaves to time in Western society.

Honoring Sabbath is saying no; time is sacred. But what should this time be set aside for?

PRACTICING SABBATH

When we read the New Testament, we see the purpose, heart, and mission behind Sabbath changes as the Christian church matures. A lot of people think Sabbath is being quiet, praying all day, or just completely vegging out on the couch. While that can be a part of Sabbath if done right, I'd argue that it can be anti-Sabbath. A quiet, miserable day of beating yourself up over all your sins, isolating yourself (and alienating others) while you pray, or just killing time until Sunday is over is actually anti-Sabbath.

When you look at the Bible as a whole, two principles pop up in relation to the Sabbath. The first is that Sabbath can only be understood when we go back and listen to the garden echo. The Sabbath is a rhythm deeply woven into the cosmos. It's part of creation's DNA. God didn't rest because he needed rest; Genesis 2 tells us the rest was a celebration, an inauguration. A day of filling the earth with his presence.

So if God on the first Sabbath flooded the earth with his presence to both signify the completion of creation and to have a day to especially fuse himself to that creation, then it only makes sense to celebrate it the same way.

What if one day a week we filled the earth with God's presence, being creative with our wallets, time, and energy? Sacred time to serve and love. I can't say Alyssa and I do this one well, but we're learning.

Maybe you invite your neighbor over for dinner on the Sabbath. Maybe you see a widow down the street and ask if you can help around the house one day a week.

Maybe entering into rest means working on the Sabbath. But if you've ever done something for others and remarked how it "filled you up" after the fact, you'll realize that's exactly in line with what Sabbath is supposed to be.

My favorite definition of the Sabbath is from Abraham Heschel: "A reminder of every man's royalty; an abolition of the distinction of master and slave, rich and poor, success and failure. To celebrate the Sabbath is to experience one's ultimate independence of civilization and society, of achievement and anxiety. The Sabbath is an embodiment of the belief that all men are equal and that equality of men means the nobility of men. The greatest sin of man is to forget that he is a prince."[4]

Notice how all the things that the world usually says make us unequal are things that have to do with work—how much money we make, what kind of cars we drive, and what our jobs are. But on the Sabbath we are all equalized. Once a week we get to shatter the idea that we are on different levels. We are all human image-bearers of God, and everyone (while resting) is the same; we are reminded that is God's ultimate heart.

When my wife and I were prayed over and encouraged and loved, that was Sabbath. That was filling the moment with God's presence just as he did in the garden. It's ripping heaven down to earth and letting the moment be sacred. Sabbath is a day we can encourage others. Who could you text with a message of appreciation?

Are your days being filled, or are you always being drained? We need to set aside time for filling.

One really fascinating thing I don't hear many preachers talk about is that even though the Sabbath was the seventh day of creation, it was Adam and Eve's *first* day of life.

Put yourself in Adam's shoes. He wasn't there for the moon and the stars. The animals. The plants. He was the crowning act of creation. When God breathed life into his nostrils, he became a living being. Then God rested. From Adam's perspective, the first full day he saw as a human was a day of rest. The day of filling.

God did all the work, and Adam got to start with rest. Only after he'd been properly filled could he live up to his vocation as a garden-cultivating image-bearer. For God it was six days of work and then rest, but for Adam his first day was rest, and only then could he truly work. That sounds a lot like the cross, doesn't it? Jesus does all the work, and we are called to enter into that rest. Our first day, the first moment we open our eyes, is supposed to be a day and moment of rest.

Is the Sabbath seen as a beginning to the week or an end to the week? A lot of us, if we are working anxiously, can't wait to have a day off. That is fine, but I've noticed a different depth about my walk with Jesus every week when I set the precedent of observing the spirit of Sabbath. Start with rest, then work. Don't work, then hope to get rest.

The Sabbath evolves after the exodus. After God takes the Israelites out of Egypt, he gives them the Torah. The Sabbath commandment is first found in Exodus 31, but it is revisited in Deuteronomy 5. There God explains that it's because they are to remember that God brought them out of their slavery in Egypt.

He tells them to take a day off every seven days because they are no longer slaves. They are free.

The second principle regarding the Sabbath is that it is to remind us that we are free.

If we aren't sabbathing, the question is, are we free? Or are we slaves to performance, to our phones, to being needed, to being in the know, to pleasure, to addiction?

The Sabbath is a day to celebrate and remember we are free people. We aren't under the empire anymore; we are under the kingdom. We aren't commodities; we are people. We aren't brickmakers; we are image-bearers. And when we remember, we free ourselves to have true community.

When we are commodities, other humans are competition.

When we rest, other humans are neighbors.

Growing up I always thought that if I wanted to be a Christian, I'd have to give up on fun. It was dismal, dark, and sacrificial. It is at times, but on the flip side it's also a faith of celebration. Christianity is one huge party. He's here! God is among us! Look what he's done! He's saved us! So let's celebrate. And sabbathing is doing exactly that. It is setting aside one day a week to party. To dance. To eat. To sing. And to love.

The Sabbath command is the fourth command. It looks back on the three about God and looks forward to the last six about how to treat people. It's the link between honoring God and loving people. And a true party does both of those things. It honors God, and it honors people.

Whenever Alyssa and I have a special dinner, we've started doing a prayer and a toast. A prayer to honor God, and a toast to look our guests and friends in the eyes and honor them. Sometimes it's nothing more than just saying we're thankful they are in our lives. But even a small dose of love can bring life in the same way the tiniest match can bring light in a dark room.

The Sabbath is a gift. It's a filling. It's not a burden or a legality meant to be technically obeyed. It's a day when we jump into God's presence headfirst and don't worry every five seconds about whether or not we are breaking it.

Simply put, Sabbath is a calling for delight.

If we know that at the full restoration of all things everything will be made new, there will be pleasures forevermore, there will be a feast and table we sit at with Jesus, then Sabbath is making that true right now. Sabbath is ripping that future delight right here into this moment. That's why a great meal is such a beautiful act of Sabbath worship. It's pleasure. It's delight.

I love the idea that Sabbath is simply about play. True play. Remember when you were a little kid and you played? You'd go out into the neighborhood, think of incredibly creative games when all you had was a can or a stick, and come back right before it got dark? That childlike sense of play is an echo of eternity. When you're playing, you're right next to the heart of God. You're tasting the future, because ultimately that's what the new heavens and new earth will be like. There will be worship of Jesus, and in that worship will be true enjoyment forever, knowing this is what we were created for, and that will be play.

In Matthew, Jesus says to enter the kingdom we have to become like little children. And I'd say one of the biggest markers of children, that isn't always true of adults, is they know how to play. Don't lose that. It's a signpost to the great feast where we are guests of the King.

Do you treat the Sabbath as a day of delight or a day of boredom? What fills you up? What gives you delight? What makes you feel new?

Whatever your answer—if it's in line with the new heavens and earth ethic—then do that thing. Paint. Eat. Laugh. Hike.

That's Sabbath, and that's worship. That's the freedom to delight as a follower of Jesus.

SIX

WORSHIP: REFLECTING GOD'S GLORY

In the garden of Eden, human beings were put in a unique space. We were below the Creator and above the creation. We were created in God's image, meaning we had a capacity no one else did. We have the weight of reflecting the very person who spun the earth into existence. God gave us that capacity.

The best way I've ever heard this explained is that we are like mirrors slanted 45 degrees. We were created to stand in this middle place. God's glory, love, and likeness shine down on us, and like any slanted mirror should, we reflect that goodness and beauty out into the world.

It works backward too. As image-bearers, our job is to be gardeners as Adam was before he ate the fruit. We are to take raw materials, make something creative and beautiful, and then offer that to God as worship. A gardener shapes, cultivates, plants, and ultimately brings value to something that before had no value.

To take sounds of instruments and make music.

To take vegetables and herbs and make a beautiful meal.

To take paint and canvas and make art.

That's also the definition of a priest—someone who takes something and offers it as praise on behalf of others to God. Our job is to take the world, beauty out of chaos, and offer it back to God as worship.

God in the garden called us to cultivate by holding that mirror at a 45-degree angle. It's a two-way thing. Something comes down and reflects out, and something comes from out and reflects up. When we reflect the beauty and goodness of the Creator out into the world, we are fulfilling this, and when we take the world and offer it through that mirror up to God, we are doing this as well.

Worship—living as mirrors that reflect God's glory—is a key part of following Jesus. It's a key part of living as a Christian.

But the minute Adam and Eve ate the fruit, that mirror shattered. It still might give a reflection of some sort, but we all know broken mirrors certainly don't give *accurate* reflections. We no longer reflect God, but are like broken shards of glass reflecting that very first sin: the desire to be like God. We reflect evil, chaos, power, greed, corruption, addiction.

And it can all be traced back to worship. When sin happened and the cosmos broke, a vacuum was created. Before the fall, our life was in shalom. We were in a flourishing garden and earth with beauty, art, and amazing color. We were fully human. We knew God and walked with him in the garden. We were orbiting around God and everything he offers—goodness, beauty, peace, and rhythm.

But when the fracture happened, that center of

ours became void. It got replaced. And like any good vacuum, stuff started getting sucked into that center. God was no longer in our hearts, so it was easy to let the first thing we came across take his place. We took the creation and elevated it above the Creator. The very things we were created to dominate now dominate us. The things we were to create and cultivate now enslave us and rule us. The rule of the garden had been reversed. We no longer had dominion. We had slavery.

That is still happening today. Everything is vying for our attention. Everything is asking for our all: Sex. Beauty. Security. Athletics. Money. Self-worth. Searching for these outside of God becomes our everything.

That's the definition of an idol: something that promises to fulfill what only God truly can. It calls on our good desires—for love, intimacy, fullness, purpose—but then turns them from a good thing to a god thing. It puts the fulfillment of desire on a throne and then becomes our master.

WE ARE STATUES SENT FROM THE CAPITAL

When ancient capital cities are excavated, it is rare to find statues of whatever god or king ruled there. Rome, for example, had hardly any statues of Caesar.

Most statues of rulers were found in the colonies, far away from the capital.

Statues, or images, are a way of saying who is in charge. Whether it's a huge statue or a face on a coin, the people know who their lord is when they see his face—even in a place he may never have visited. The statue set up in a colony one thousand miles from Rome was a way of saying "Caesar is lord." It served as a reflection and reminder.

And so are we. We are living, breathing statues on earth as image-bearers of who is in charge. The problem, though, is that unlike statues, we can turn around and say no.

No, I don't want to worship you. No, I don't want to represent you. No, I don't want to reflect you. That's when the Bible uses phrases like God "gave us over" to false gods, idols, and worship of the creation instead of the Creator.

There are two significant consequences every time we make that decision: (1) we are no longer able to properly reflect him, and (2) we become like the idols we worship.

Think about the statues again in the colonies. If for some reason Rome "gave up" on a colony and let it be, and it no longer maintained or cleaned the statues, they would deteriorate and crumble.

Imagine Rome writing off a few statues and no longer taking care of them or "giving them over" to themselves. Those statues would quickly turn to rubble, piles of marble or stone. They would no longer properly represent Rome, the very source of their existence.

When we decide to worship something besides God, that same thing happens with us. We begin to lose the thing that makes us human. Our humanness begins to crumble. As image-bearers we have weight, but when we abdicate that responsibility, we lose that weight. Our glory begins to fall. We become ruins of what he created us to be.

Now, of course, we never fully lose that image while we are alive. No matter how hard you scratch, gnaw, or pull, you can't get the image of God off of you fully. There's still glory residue no matter how hard you try. But the principle that is impossible to escape is we can't be image neutral—we *will* reflect or become more and more like something or someone.

When heaven crashes down onto earth, it looks like we are reflecting and imaging God's very own self in us. But to keep God from coming close, the only thing we have to do is worship something else as ultimate. Like the statues, this immediately cuts us off from the source and takes away our humanness.

It's a scary question but one that should be asked: What would you be like if the thing that made you human—the image and likeness of God—was taken away from you?

In C. S. Lewis's novel *The Great Divorce*, hell is painted as a picture of what happens when that image is fully removed. Heaven is inhabited by "solid people" and hell is inhabited by "ghosts." There is a weight in heaven that is so real, so thick, it's painful to the ghosts. In hell, they live hundreds of miles away from the nearest person. And hell is airy, thin, ghostlike. But heaven is dense, huge in proportion to hell. The bodies have weight, as if they were made for that place.

When the people in hell visit heaven, even the blades of grass are too dense to walk on. It's painful to them because they have been *dehumanized*. By wanting to worship themselves and other things, the very thing that made them truly human (namely God's reflected image in them) was scratched away. "Reality is harsh to the feet of shadows."[1] They don't have that image in them. They don't have that weight of glory. They are now subhuman. Sub-images.

And that's the logical conclusion of idolatry. It's colluding with evil to wipe away our humanness and to worship things that are not God. If we want to live our lives refusing the image of God in us, which is also the very thing that makes us human, hell becomes the place where God finally says okay. Which leads us to the second consequence: when God is no longer the image we orbit, then we become like whatever takes his place.

WE ALL WORSHIP SOMETHING

When I was at my non-Christian college, Jesus was fairly attractive to people in my circle. They enjoyed hearing about his grace and had no qualms about some of his teachings, but they usually got upset when they realized Jesus asked for everything.

When they'd see those passages about Jesus telling people to give up everything, say goodbye to all they know, they'd get upset.

How dare he. Who does he think he is?

They'd always freak out because they thought Jesus had no right to ask for everything from them. To ask them to put their whole lives, desires, and passions at his feet.

I never got why they *only* got mad at Jesus for that. Jesus isn't the only one who asks for everything. In fact, *everything* asks for everything.

Everything asks for your life. For your all. For every last drop of your allegiance.

Power does. Sexual fulfillment does. Athletics do. Your significant other does. Your job does. Jesus isn't unique in that way. But he is unique in that he gave up everything first. All those other things use fear and false promises and force to get what they want.

Jesus is the only one who lays down his life for you first, before he asks for yours. He pursues, he dies, he gives up everything, and then calls us to himself. There's no force, only wooing. His love is so great that it *compels* us to lay down our lives in return. That's the only appropriate response when we understand just how great his sacrifice was for us.

God's heart in Psalm 115 tells us that he draws idolatry out to its logical conclusion: "Their idols are silver and gold, / the work of human hands. / They have mouths, but do not speak."[2]

God even makes the point that when we cry out to idols, they can't save us. They're dead. The paradox of an idol, unlike Jesus, is that the worshiper gives it power. We are the ones who give it life. Alcohol can only be a god if we make it one. Money can only be a god if we worship it. But Jesus is King and Lord regardless of what we do.

He's someone worth giving my life to.

Some of us instead still settle for idols, even though we don't realize it. We laugh at the imagery of the Old Testament as if we are more enlightened and would never do anything so foolish. Yet nothing has changed, except for the clothes the idols wear.

When's the last time that bottle of alcohol really satisfied? When's the last time it forgave you? Gave you joy? Fully loved you? It can't. We crafted it with our own hands.

What a lot of people don't realize is that an idol can be anything. It can be good things like relationships or work. The problem is, even good things can become "god" things.

Young people are especially tempted to orbit their lives around significant others. Suddenly a switch flips in the heart, and we begin to get our satisfaction, worth, and identity from that person.

God is against idols because when the pieces of life are in their proper places, we can enjoy him and those things best. When we make another person an idol, we end up squeezing the life out of them. Only one person has the ability to sustain being God, and that's Jesus.

When we worship Jesus, we can love that person even more because our center isn't tied to or defined by them. If they upset us, rather than being affected negatively every time, we can give back love, grace, and forgiveness because our self-worth comes from God.

It also doesn't work because people die. I heard a pastor say that one day when his wife dies, he will certainly grieve and be devastated, but he doesn't want to walk before the casket and say, "There's my god. My god is dead." Being anchored in Jesus is the only way he'd be able to get through something like that.

Idols are fickle. Be it a person, alcohol, sex, anything—they all make for cruel gods. For me, baseball was a particularly unstable god. My average went up and down. My performance swayed. I had good days, and I had bad days. It was ruthless when I didn't perform, and easy when I did. Sounds a lot like the schizophrenic gods of ancient times that people always worried they would anger. Yet God is constant. Always forgiving. Always loving. Never changing.

One of the biggest traits of an idol is that we are blinded to it. It seems normal to us.

That's the allure and power of an idol—we usually don't know we have one unless it gets attacked or taken away. The easiest way to find an idol is to poke it. If it's an idol, it'll show its teeth. It'll bark back. They always do.

But Jesus doesn't need defending. He never defended himself but gave himself as an offering, and in the process defeated evil—in a moment when everyone thought evil had won!

Charles Spurgeon said it best: "The gospel is like a caged lion. It does not need to be defended, it just needs to be let out of its cage." The mystery of Jesus is just like the mystery in Revelation 5. He's *called* the Lion of Judah, but when John looked, he *saw* a lamb slaughtered. Jesus is a powerful, victorious lion who achieved that victory by the act of the lamb who was slain.

May we be people who, similar to the creatures around the throne in Revelation, worship the Lamb and sing his praise: "To him who sits on the throne and to the Lamb / be blessing and honor and glory and might forever and ever!"[3]

SEVEN

GOD'S KINGDOM: HEAVEN ON EARTH

Son of God.

King of kings.

Lord of lords.

Those were titles for a man who lived two thousand years ago. He was even called a savior because he was to bring peace to the world. He was divine and human, and they even argued that our calendars should revolve around him. The only problem is, this man is dead and so is his kingdom.

His name? Caesar Augustus.

Were you thinking of someone else?[1]

That was the atmosphere of the first century. All sorts of people were promising peace, order, and security; but only the Caesar had a right to do so. When Jesus declared he was Lord and he was King, the effect was explosive, revolutionary, and offensive. Because if Jesus was King, that implied Caesar *was not*.

A kingdom is any place ruled by a king. It's a space of ruling, reigning, and governmental authority. Jesus was saying that God's kingdom—the place where God reigns and rules—had now crash-landed in himself. He was the God of Israel, visiting his people and fulfilling the promise to establish his reign and rule in their midst.

A lot of times we think the kingdom of God is something highly spiritual or fluffy. But it has a weight and a force to it, even if it is peaceful. Jesus' grace, mercy, and love were heavy. And when he unleashed them through his death and resurrection, there was a ripple. It was God himself saying, "I'm now in charge, and my reign is being ushered in." Anyone in his path couldn't help but get hit by the power of love, grace, and healing.

There is power in the kingdom.

The good news of the Bible is that when you step into God's kingdom and under his authority, everything changes.

Christianity isn't about going to heaven when you die; it's about making heaven true on earth in every facet and level of our relationship with God, others, and self. The Christian life is asking, how can I make what's true of Jesus and his gospel true in whatever aspect of my life?

That's what it means for Jesus to be Lord in your life. To put our whole lives under God's reign, and live as a new humanity, a community that points to the future restoration of all things.

THE LAST SHALL BE FIRST

It was a Sunday afternoon right after I'd finished speaking to a youth group. The youth pastor and his wife were asking us to lunch after the service, but I quickly jumped in and said no. Alyssa then gave me that look. *Why can't we go out to lunch with them?* I couldn't really produce a good reason, except that Alyssa and I had already planned to picnic that day.

The truth was, I intended to propose to her in just a couple of hours.

I still remember the moment. I had two of my buddies go ahead of me to the location—a nice little private beach area overlooking Puget Sound. I had them go a few hours before to set up everything. I printed out every picture we had ever taken in our relationship and had one of them post those on the fence leading down to the beach, along with rose petals and candles. My other buddy set up a couple of cameras too. (I'm a YouTuber—I have to record everything.) I felt like a secret service agent: I even had a microphone taped under my shirt the whole time.

I had this grand picture in my mind, but when I got to the moment, I was so awkward. I had all this stuff I wanted to say, but literally could barely get any of it out. I think it's the only time in my life when I've been at a loss for words and stumbled through sentences I'm not even sure were English.

One thing I did was read a journal entry "to my future wife" that I'd written a couple of years before and told Alyssa I believed that was her. Then I got out a thermos of hot water and a bowl and proceeded to wash Alyssa's feet.

It sounds sweet, but honestly it was kind of awkward. Do I just take the washcloth and rub her feet? Do I get in the nooks and crannies and make sure they are totally clean? Is my washing them telling her that her feet are dirty and they need cleaning?

In reality, when I was washing her feet, I told her I wanted this to be a symbol of our relationship. I wanted to serve her, love her, and cherish her. It was a moment I won't forget.

But I haven't always kept that promise. There are times I'm selfish, impatient, and unloving, and I have to return again and again to that foot washing. That service. That love.

Functionally, foot washing made a lot more sense in first-century Palestine since everyone was usually wearing retro Birkenstocks. Their feet would get filthy from the dust and whatever else was left scattered on paths and streets.

Because of the nature of foot washing, especially in a Jewish culture of daily and ritual cleanliness, it was even beneath Jewish slaves to wash someone's feet. Most prominent Jews had a slave at the door who would untie your sandals, but it was usually reserved for the person himself to wash his own feet with water provided by the host.

So you can see just how lowly and scandalous Jesus' actions are in John 13. Toward the end of his life, he was having a meal with his disciples and then took off his outer garments, tied a towel around his waist, poured water into a basin, and began to wash his disciples' feet.[2]

That'd be like the president of the United States taking off his suit, getting on his hands and knees, and washing your feet after a long hike in the mountains. It would feel weird and inappropriate. We probably would react the same way Peter did and refuse it.

But Jesus insisted. He even went on to tell Peter that if he didn't let him wash Peter's feet, then Peter had no part in him. When Jesus was done, he said, "A servant is not greater than his master, nor is a messenger greater than the one who sent him."[3]

I think washing someone's feet holds the same shock value today as it did two thousand years ago, and so we shouldn't be afraid to do it from time to time for friends, enemies, and in moments where we want to disturb and disrupt people to cause them to ask us about Jesus. But I also think foot washing can be metaphorical.

Essentially, it's serving. It's taking the lowest seat and doing what others won't. Jesus clearly states that the kingdom of God operates and sees power differently than the world. According to Jesus, the "powerful" are the servants. The ones who make themselves last.

I'm challenged to live this out every day of my

marriage. For twenty-three years I was conditioned to see that life was about my priorities, my goals, and the other details of my life. Yet Jesus strangely says if we want to find our lives and find joy, we have to lose them. We have to give them up. There are moments, I wish more often, when I sit and rest in Jesus and am able to turn to Alyssa and serve her.

For the longest time, we argued over making the bed. To Alyssa it's what starts the day and makes the day feel right. It gives a joy and attitude about the day. I think it's ridiculous because I have a tough time doing something I know will get messed up every twenty-four hours for the rest of my life.

But I finally decided to put my arguments aside and simply serve Alyssa. Even though it's something really small, I understand what Jesus was talking about. There's this strange joy that begins to come. After I make the bed, I do admit it looks nice, but more important, it does something for Alyssa. She feels loved, cherished, and valued. It creates this dynamic and spirit about our relationship that fills us, gives us joy, and brings us just a tiny bit closer together.

It even produces this dance-like rhythm in our marriage in which we are mutually serving and dancing with each other in love. And if you've been in that spot, you know that's the spot we were created for. That's the kingdom.

What could you do today or tomorrow that hoists the kingdom flag of serving? I think drastic things specifically have a way of shocking people out of their worldview and making them, even for a second, ask, why? We talk a lot about Jesus, but if we washed some more feet, more people might start following him.

THE SWORD OR THE CROSS

One thing that stood in stark contrast to Rome was that the kingdom of Jesus seemed to think self-giving love could conquer enemies, while Rome thought killing that enemy would do the trick.

It's hard to read the New Testament and not think America looks a lot more like the empire of Rome than the kingdom of Jesus. I agree with N. T. Wright: "When God wants to change the world, he doesn't send in the tanks. He sends in the meek, the mourners, those who are hungry and thirsty for God's justice, the peacemakers, and so on."[4]

If we are to be people of the light, we should study history. Looking back, it's easy to see the empire that thought it could get what it wanted by killing people doesn't exist anymore. The kingdom that thought it could transform people's lives by loving them still exists—and is growing.

Some might say, "Well, Jesus' world was different than ours." To which I'd answer, "You're right; it was way worse."

The Jewish people technically had been back from exile for almost five hundred years by the time of Jesus. They were in their own land. Yet for almost that entire period, outside of a few blips on the radar, the Persian, Greek, or Roman empires ruled them all but about twenty-five of those years. For the Jewish people, this indicated something was deeply wrong. God had promised to establish his reign and rule and do something new and explosive in Israel. If Cyrus or Alexander the Great or Caesar were still ruling Judea, then that meant it hadn't happened yet.

The Jewish people were anxiously waiting for a leader to rise up. To do what they had read about in the Prophets: crush the enemies, defeat the occupying country, and establish Israel as its own sovereign nation again.

When was God going to establish his kingdom for Israel and the faithful?

Little did they know he was about to do that very thing, but in a radically different way than anyone expected.

A lot of people figured this would happen through—you guessed it—physical violence. That's how it happened in the Old Testament, and that's how Judas Maccabeus attempted it two hundred years earlier. Because that's simply the only way to get rid of a foreign occupier.

And yet Jesus radically opposed that violence. In fact, in every instance that killing the enemy becomes a viable option for the followers of Jesus in the gospels, Jesus flatly condemns it.

When Peter cuts off a man's ear to protect Jesus, he's rebuked harshly.

When Jesus triumphantly enters Jerusalem, he cries because Jerusalem didn't know the things "that make for peace."[5]

When Jesus is arrested and taken to a Roman execution device, he seems to give up with no fight.

When two disciples ask to be placed at his left and right in his kingdom (they thought Jesus was going to violently take the temple back and establish his earthly rule), he says they clearly do not know what they are asking.

It was clear by the fact he was gaining and attracting such large crowds that people thought God's long-awaited promise to crush Rome and establish Israel forever was coming true in Jesus. And so Jesus very quickly goes right to the people's hearts.

He puts his cards on the table in the very first sermon in Matthew, famously called the Sermon on the Mount. Which, by the way, wasn't just potent teaching, but was set up by Matthew to tell the reader, "This is the new Torah! This is the new Law! This is the manifesto for Jesus followers!" It isn't just a nice teaching that we can put on a coffee cup but something we are responsible to live out if we call ourselves Jesus followers.

Jesus explicitly addresses the Old Testament way of doing things: "You have heard that it was said, 'You shall love your neighbor and hate your enemy.' But I say to you, Love your enemies and pray for those who persecute you, so that you may be sons of your Father who is in heaven."[6]

Jesus is saying, "I know you've heard it a certain way. I know you think that way is right. But if you want to be a part of this movement turning the world upside down and living in my kingdom, then you need to love your enemies." He even goes so far as to say if someone slaps you, turn the other cheek. If they take your tunic, give them your cloak.

With that in mind, can you imagine how ridiculous the cross must have looked to any faithful Jew living in Israel in the first century? Rather than being the moment of victory, the cross proved the very opposite. A crucified Messiah isn't a Messiah at all. All the hopes of Jesus restoring the kingdom of Israel were crushed the minute the Romans drove nails into his wrists and feet. All the followers of Jesus thought they had wasted the past three years of their lives.

Israel was occupied for so long they almost couldn't remember what it meant to be in their own land without anyone else running the show. Yet, in that moment, love strangely won. Jesus, even in the middle of the execution, said while on the cross, "Father, forgive them, for they know not what they do" (Luke 23:34).

Jesus could have easily crushed the opposition. He could have easily called down an army of angels to absolutely slaughter everyone who oppressed and hurt Israel. Instead, he knew the way to change the world was through sacrificing his own life—and he calls us to do the same. That's a strong task and a strong call, but if we are Jesus followers, that's the path carved for us. Sacrificial love, giving one's life on behalf of another, is the way of our Lord and must be our way too. It's one of the most defining marks of a Jesus-kingdom citizen.

As pastor Brian Zahnd put it, "Ultimately we cannot eliminate enemies through violence—violence only multiplies enemies. The only way to eliminate enemies is to love them, forgive them."[7]

What if you could defeat evil itself? What if the force, the spirit, the evil behind all tangible evil could be destroyed? Would you? Of course you would.

The truth is, that's already happened, according to claims of a first-century rabbi in Judea. And he said it had already happened, get this, when he was executed by the Romans and resurrected three days later.

That is the most explosive, countercultural,

ridiculous thing I've ever heard. Jesus said he defeated evil in a six-hour event that left him in agony, bloodied to a pulp, and dangling from a piece of wood. That's the foolishness of the cross Paul talks about in 1 Corinthians.

And if Jesus said that and modeled that, the question becomes, do we really trust him that the Jesus way is *the* way?

For thousands of years Jesus followers have altered history, changed cultures, and left lasting legacies simply because they believed this to be true.

When they were thrown to lions and had their bodies ripped—no, chewed—apart, they bled love, not hatred.

When Peter was crucified, he didn't pull out the sword as he did on the night of Jesus' arrest; he asked to be crucified upside down because he wasn't worthy of dying in the same way as his Lord.

Enemy love changes the world. Enemy love breaks and transforms hearts. Enemy love makes people look to Jesus. And enemy love is nonnegotiable in the kingdom.

This topic brings up loads of practical questions that space here won't allow, and also because I don't know the answers to a lot of those questions. But the big question is, are we even having this conversation? Are we wrestling?

This concept isn't one that's nice and tidy. It

deserves creative solutions. I'm learning day by day to really trust that Jesus knew what he was doing. He can be trusted. His way is the way of the future like we talked about in chapter 4.

It is foolishness to the world, but somehow the mysterious heart of God says this is the way, and looking back on church history, time and time again radical love does defeat evil.

THANKFULNESS IS THE SECRET

Foot washing and enemy love aren't the only markers of a kingdom citizen. Thankfulness, too, is a badge that should mark us as Jesus followers.

For the longest time I thought God wanted me to do something super-spiritual for him if I was going to follow him and do "big" things. I believed in order for God to really like me, I needed to do something crazy for him, such as move to Africa or heal cancer.

But the apostle Paul, on multiple occasions, says stuff like, "And whatever you do, in word or deed, do everything in the name of the Lord Jesus, giving thanks to God the Father through him."[8]

Or to Timothy he says, "For everything created by God is good, and nothing is to be rejected if it is received with thanksgiving, for it is made holy by the word of God and prayer."[9]

In another place he even says to give thanks in all circumstances.[10]

I think thanksgiving is the secret to a healthy Christian life. When we feel as if we earned something, we become entitled and smug. But if we understand even the oxygen in our lungs is a gift from an amazing and beautiful Creator, then gratitude and thankfulness start to explode in our lives. When we can be thankful, we get joy.

Author Ann Voskamp has written beautifully about the art of thanksgiving in her book *One Thousand Gifts*. She kept a running list of everything she was thankful for, big and small, and she noticed it unlocked something in her heart.

The best part about thanksgiving is we can do it anywhere. I thought I had to do big things for God, but when I started to really read the New Testament, I realized God wasn't as concerned with me doing big things as he was with my attitude in the middle of the thing I was already in. I didn't have to be a pastor or a theologian to be more holy. Holiness happens when thanksgiving happens, and I can do that if I'm typing, writing, cooking, walking, or playing sports.

What if you took your life as it is now and, rather than thinking you had to do something more spiritual or holy, just infused a ton of thanksgiving right there in the middle of it?

Thanksgiving has also been a way to show what

things I should do and what things I should steer
clear from. It's a lot easier to know what might be a
sinful or poor decision in my life when I can't give
thanks for it.

I can't thank God that I stole a car, and I can't
thank God when I lie to a friend because I know those
aren't things he orchestrated or provided. If you can't
give thanks for something, then that's a good sign you
probably shouldn't be doing it.

And the question we always have to ask is, *what's
it like in heaven right now and how do I make this true
on earth?*

In Scripture we see heaven isn't far away; it's simply
God's dimension. His space. Isaiah, the Gospels, and
Revelation give us a peek behind the curtain, where
we see worship and thanksgiving. Thanking God for
what he's done, what he's doing, and what he's about
to do. And in that moment when we are thankful to
and worship him, we fulfill the very core of the kingdom prayer.

Growing up, I often heard the Lord's Prayer
recited, and for some reason it always sounded as if
people were reading it at a funeral—dry, dead, and
monotone.

Yet at the center of the prayer, it says, "Your kingdom come, your will be done, on earth as it is in
heaven."

Jewish folks in Jesus' day would bring emphasis

to something by describing the same thing two different ways. Scholars argue that's what is going on: your kingdom come, your will be done. So where is God's kingdom coming? Simple: anywhere his will is being done.

And notice again how Jesus is teaching his followers to pray that the kingdom would come. Not leave, but come. Right here. Right now. In our midst.

And then it says, "On earth as it is in heaven." Make true on earth what is true in heaven.

Death isn't true in heaven, so we should be people of life here.

There's no bitterness in heaven, so we should forgive people here.

There's only a beautiful flourishing life in heaven, so we should make that happen here.

What if we really took that prayer to heart? What if we really believed it? What if we prayed it every morning?

I hung a wood-pallet art piece right above my computer to remind me: "Your kingdom come, your will be done, on earth as it is in heaven." I want that prayer to be at the forefront of my mind. When I see evil, I want to pray that his kingdom would come. When I see hurt, I want to pray that his kingdom would come.

One little exercise I've started doing recently is replacing the word *earth* with the city I live in: "Your kingdom come, your will be done, in Kihei as it is in heaven." That makes it so much more real to me. The fun part is it makes me restudy the Bible and ask, how do I do this? What does heaven look like? What does God's space and dimension look like? What does the reign of Jesus look like, and how can I make that come by the power of the Spirit here in my city?

Do you pray that prayer? Do you have that heart for your city? What would it look like if you prayed that God's kingdom would exist in New York as it does in heaven? If you made that the cry of your heart?

EIGHT

BROKENNESS: TAKING OFF THE MASK

had just moved in with my aunt and uncle while attending community college, and I was sitting on their couch about midday, ugly-face crying. If you've done the same, you know what I'm talking about. It's where a cry session turns the corner and becomes a full-blown weep.

I was really struggling at that time with a bunch of things—depression, things I'd done wrong, disenchantment and disillusionment with this whole Jesus-following thing. I finally broke and shared all the hurt, pain, and ache I had been holding on to.

It was the first time I had been really honest and taken off my mask. Whether it was friends asking how I was doing and always answering with the cliché "Fine," or those dark thoughts I always had of *If people knew the real me, they'd run as fast as they could in the opposite direction*, I constantly played the game of projecting a certain version of myself.

I can't describe the sense of freedom I had when weights fell off my shoulders in that moment. I remember my aunt and uncle just listening, encouraging, and reminding me how much God loved me. It was truly healing.

Maybe you haven't heard this before—I know it took me a long time to realize it—but that kind of brokenness is essential to this thing called Christianity.

WOUNDS OR SCARS?

We all have wounds—things that make us physically cringe just thinking about them. They could have been caused by something we've done or something that's been done against us; regardless, emotional wounds are sensitive.

For me, there are all the poor choices I made in high school and college that to this day haunt me when I'm not focusing on grace and Jesus. Or memories of growing up in a household with only one parent, when most of my friends had traditional families. Or tough breakups that give you that sense of searing pain that not much else does.

The problem with wounds, though, is that our first inclination is to cover them. We think if we just slap a bandage on, it'll heal by itself. And sometimes that might be true, but when it's a really bad wound, that only makes it worse. No one can see it, but it's festering. If left untreated, a covered wound can get an infection, which, if bad enough, could even kill you. Oxygen and daylight are some of the first steps to healing a wound.

What if that's what it's like when we don't deal with the wounds in our hearts? Nelson Mandela reminded us, "Resentment is like drinking poison and then hoping it will kill your enemies." Resentment or bitterness is a symptom of a spiritual wound. We get angry. We lash out. If you touch a wound, people coil back and cringe because it's so sensitive.

What would someone have to touch in your life for you to react like that? To recoil? To cringe?

What if God wants to heal that? What if he wants to turn your wounds into scars?

The interesting thing about scars is that we don't hide scars as we do wounds. Wounds we cover; we mask; we make sure no one can see or touch. Scars are the opposite. We aren't afraid to show our scars because they tell a story.[1]

I have a little tiny scar on my upper lip because I thought it'd be a great idea to eat a dog's food when I was a year old. The dog didn't think it was so genius, and he bit me in the face.

I have a one-inch clean scar on my right knuckle. I found my mom's pocketknife as a kid, took it into a hiding place, and began playing with it. Of course, I wasn't too sure what it did so I tested it on my pointer finger. It sliced me right open.

Scars tell stories. And for the most part, if people see a scar, they ask about it, and we are not afraid to tell them. Because they don't hurt anymore. You can touch any of my scars, and they don't hurt; I don't cringe or pull back. It's just an opportunity for me to tell you what happened and how it's been healed.

What if Jesus wants to take our wounds and turn them into scars? We don't have to be ashamed of them anymore. We can bring them to the Healer (a name God calls himself in Exodus 15:26).

Sometimes, though, it's not that easy. Some wounds get healed the minute we come to Jesus, while others are a lot harder to walk through.

And it's in those moments I have to remember two things.

First, I can't buy the lie that God doesn't care or is aloof in those moments. He's not distant or far away. He's right there in the middle of the guilt, revolting thoughts, and self-condemnation. He's whispering.

He's there. He knows. He heals. He comes close.

Second, I have to remind myself that past mistakes are not the truest things about me. It's just phantom pain. Someone who has lost an arm, a leg, or some part of his body might experience *phantom pain*. It's when you feel sharp pain in a part of your body you don't even have anymore.

This phantom pain is not real even though brain synapses are firing and telling the person it is. I can't imagine how hard in that moment it is to believe it isn't real, even when you're able to look down and see you have no left foot. The pain is so sharp and vivid. But at the end of the day, the pain is simply not true.

I think that's a lot like what we feel in those regretful moments. When the same sin or same grief or same guilt keeps replaying, or when we drive by something that reminds us of it, or see something on Facebook that shoots a sharp guilt pain through our bodies, we have to remind ourselves that's phantom pain. It's not real. It's not the truest thing about us. In God's dimension, heaven, he has declared that when we follow him we are new. We are clean. We are forgiven. We are his children. He delights over us. He isn't distant, but near.

And *those* are the truest things about us. Not the voice of the wound. We can put our feet down in that moment, cry out for help, hang on tightly, and keep reminding ourselves that's not real. It's a scar. It's been healed.

Jesus says so, and we can trust him because he's been there. He knows what it's like to be hurt, bruised, and beaten, and to ache. He knows what it's like to be betrayed and abandoned. He knows what it's like to give only love but receive only hate. He knows what it's like, and no other god can claim that.

Are you letting Jesus turn your wounds into scars? What if Jesus wants to heal the dark parts in your life, so then you can turn around and tell others just how good he really is? Only when a wound is a scar will we let it tell a story. You can then point at the scar and say, "Look what Jesus did."

In Japanese culture there is a type of pottery art called *kintsugi* that deals with broken items such as clay pots, vases, and bowls. When a bowl or pot breaks, *kintsugi* artists put it back together using a lacquer mixed with either gold, silver, or platinum.

When the pot is put back together, the gold, silver, or platinum veins running through the pot exactly where it had previously been broken are the most eye-catching. The new glory of the beautiful creation is the golden-laced broken pieces that have been repaired. If you google this art form, you'll see what I'm talking about—it's remarkably beautiful.

With *kintsugi*, when something becomes broken, it doesn't become less valuable. The new golden-laced repair makes it *more* valuable. It doesn't try to hide or disguise the imperfections, but instead puts them on full display in all their beauty and glory.

I don't think we are much different when we come to Jesus. Some of the most inspiring people we know are those who have been hurt, who have suffered, or are broken, yet they still have a peace, joy, and resilience about them. Scars don't hide our history; they show it. And when we show our scars, we get to point to the Healer who wove his grace right into the depths of every crack and fragmented part in our soul.

Sometimes it's metaphorical scars, but sometimes it's physical scars. I've talked to a lot of people who have tried for years to rid themselves of shame and guilt and ache by cutting themselves. I recently talked with someone who said she cuts because "she thinks she deserves the pain."

My heart breaks when I hear that. The beauty of Jesus is that he's not asking us to hurt ourselves, inflict pain, or make ourselves worthy of him. We are already worthy because of who made us. We have inherent value because the very Creator of the universe spun us into existence, and he even dances over us![2] Thinking we have to punish ourselves to be loved is nowhere in the Bible. In fact, the opposite is claimed in the Bible.

Jesus took our pain on himself. He felt that weight, that crushing sense of ache and pain, and he bore it fully. If pain and shame were a cup, he drank it to the very last drop so that we never have to. That's why we celebrate and rejoice: because we know Jesus stepped in the gap, shouldered it all, and then turned to us with a tender glance and called us his child. We are his. We don't have to hide anymore.

If you're reading this and you deal with cutting, please know you are loved and God only wants to infuse you with grace, joy, and beauty. You don't need to do that anymore. He heals. And then you can point at the scars and say, "Look what Jesus did."

For me, sharing how Jesus has healed my past is a deeper level of healing. Whenever I talk to others, there's a solidarity, a vulnerability, because God is there and healing takes place. Don't be afraid to tell your story. Don't be afraid to show your scars. You may be able to bring light to a topic and help others who are still self-inflicting wounds.

Physical scars aren't the only type of hurting. The

most painful scars we can't visibly see come from sexual trauma.

I get a lot of pretty personal emails, probably because Alyssa and I talk about relationships on YouTube, and one thing that comes up again and again is sexual assault and rape—and the guilt, shame, and grief that come along with it.

I don't think anything can hurt us more than sexuality being robbed, stolen, distorted, or misused against us. Sexuality is so intertwined with our spirituality and our very being, so those wounds are deeper than any other. If you speak with people who have suffered abuse in this area, they'll tell you how deep the feelings of shame and regret and hurt go. Even the apostle Paul makes the point that sexual issues are different from everything else.[3]

Whatever the wound is, something deep like assault or something seemingly insignificant that still stings, know that healing comes from Jesus. He takes it, heals it, and gives new life.

RUNAWAY GOAT

There is an ancient Israelite and Jewish holiday called Yom Kippur, or the "Day of Atonement." Back when the temple still existed, the priest sacrificed one goat on an altar and sent a second goat into the wilderness.

The second goat has always fascinated me. According to the Torah, the high priest was commanded to put his hands on the head of the goat, confess Israel's sins, and transfer them to the goat. When that was done, he would send the goat out into the wilderness never to be seen again. This is where we get the term *scapegoat*.

But what's fascinating is Jesus wrapped up all these traditions in himself, and that scapegoat was only a shadow. The real thing is Jesus.

We are called to take the deepest, darkest, hardest sins of ours (ones we've done and ones that have been done against us) and reach out our hands and put them on Jesus. On the cross Jesus was both the sacrifice and the scapegoat. He took our sins into the grave, as the goat took them to the wilderness.

The beautiful part is, once we transfer them to Jesus, he leaves them in the grave, resurrects, and shuts the door to death behind him. We have new life now. We have peace and forgiveness. We are new creations.

Have you had that moment? Have you leaned in and put that weight on Jesus? Are you tired yet? Tired of the shame, guilt, and game we have to play to keep it all together? He wants it, he takes it, and he defeats it.

And notice, too, that when Jesus comes out the other side, in the resurrection, his wounds are no longer wounds.

They are scars.

They've been healed. They tell a story. What's more, after the resurrection Jesus is in a perfect glorified body. (His body is what ours will look like at the end of time when everything is fully restored.)

Yet he still has scars. While many of us see scars as a weakness, if Jesus has scars *after* the resurrection, then maybe they're not. Maybe scars make us truly human. They show we've lived. They tell our story. Without our scars we might not be the same people, but praise God they are no longer wounds.

This is illustrated perfectly after Jesus rises from the dead and interacts with Thomas, also known as the doubting disciple. His friends were telling Thomas that Jesus had risen, but Thomas didn't believe them. "Unless I see in his hands the mark of the nails, and place my finger into the mark of the nails, and place my hand into his side, I will never believe."[4]

Eight days later, Jesus and Thomas finally see each other. Jesus doesn't rebuke Thomas and tell him to believe harder. He doesn't tell him to read more apologetics books. He doesn't say, "Just have faith." He says, "Put your finger here, and see my hands; and put out your hand, and place it in my side. Do not disbelieve, but believe."[5]

The answer to Thomas's doubt was Jesus telling Thomas to reach out and touch him. To feel his scars.

It's almost as if Jesus' scars were what proved his humanity. Made him real in that moment.

Many times we miss Jesus because we try to muster intellectual rigor or arguments in our darkest times, but Jesus simply says, *"Touch me."* There's intimacy there. There's Jesus saying in our pain, *"I know. Look at my scars."* He had experienced death, but he had also experienced resurrection.

Which means evil didn't win.

NINE

FELLOWSHIP: THE POWER OF THE TABLE

In almost all cultures, except Western postmodern society, the table represents something deeply sacred.

It's a place of peace, of love, and of covenant. Sitting with others at a table aligns you with those people. Whoever is at the table together is, in one way or another, family. Some cultures take this principle so far that the leader of the home is responsible for protecting guests at the table at all expense—even if that means death. It is an honor, and hospitality is an art.

Jesus knew the power of the table and used it in some unique ways. He never just provided spiritual facts, but entered into people's lives and let truth rest at the table.

As Christians—as his followers—it's important to ask whether we do the same.

NOT A THEORY, BUT A MEAL

Jesus dying on the cross, even if you aren't a follower of Jesus, can arguably be called the most impactful event in all history. It has changed more people, affected more people, and passed through cultures and languages more than anything else. You'd think

Jesus would give quite possibly his best sermon or teaching to make sure the disciples understood what was about to happen.

He had been with them for three years and was now a mere twenty-four hours away from what it all was leading to. We would expect him to give every last drop of truth, spiritual points, and facts to the disciples to make sure they didn't miss what was coming.

When we read the account of the last night Jesus had with his disciples—men he had known well for three years—we expect to find the best sermon of his life, right? Or at least a huge all-night recap of everything he'd taught them the past three years. But there's no whiteboard, pulpit, or systematic theology book.

Jesus didn't say, "All right, disciples. Here's an outline describing atonement. You need to memorize this and make sure you understand the theological truth that's about to unfold."

He didn't do any of that. Instead, for the very last act of his life with his disciples, Jesus *ate* with them.

To describe the biggest event in human history, Jesus didn't give them a theory, a formula, or an equation; he gave them a *meal*.

He used bread and wine to describe the cross.

The table is a sacred space.

More than ever we need to learn the art of sitting at

a table with other image-bearers of God. In a culture that is constantly dehumanizing or reducing people to profile photos, job titles, and failures, the table is a chance to restore glory. I see this firsthand with every person I interact with online.

Because I'm a public figure (whatever that means), I've noticed people can say things about me on Twitter, Facebook, and other places that I'm sure they wouldn't say if they were with me in person. And not because they'd be scared to (I'm not a big guy, so I'm not scary), but because it doesn't feel right to be rude to someone in person.

When we dehumanize, we are able to dismiss, belittle, and be rude. But face-to-face, even if we disagree with someone, it's so much harder to be dismissive or rude or caricature them because there's something in us that doesn't like to make others feel bad about themselves.

The internet is changing how we interact with each other, because with the internet you can't see what your words do to someone else. You can't see the hurt in his face, hear the ache in her voice. When you do, it does something to you. It lets you empathize. Take a different posture. And lean in.

Where we are in the Western world, we need the table more than ever. Fellowship around a meal certainly isn't unique, though, and the reconciliation the table represents is needed everywhere. Everyone opposes someone else. Conservatives don't like liberals. Gays don't like Christians. Israelis don't like Palestinians. White cops don't like black teens.

Now, of course, these stereotypes aren't true across the board, but we've bought this lie and heard this narrative over and over again through media.

I'm technically Native American, but I am self-aware enough to know that I look like a white person or at least enough to get the privilege that comes with that. If Alyssa and I have a son, do you know it's twenty-one times less likely that he'd be shot and killed by a policeman than his black friend? That means twenty-one black teens would have to be killed by the cops for there to be a statistical possibility that my white son would be.

That is the kind of stuff you hear at the table. Don't be afraid to sit down and ask your neighbors, ask your enemies. Ask them to tell you how they've been hurt, judged, or maligned because of the color of their skin. Instead of assuming, ask and then listen. You'll be surprised what it'll do for your soul and for theirs.

The table isn't just a place of a meal, but a symbol of family. Of oneness. Of we-are-in-this-together-ness.

Rabbi Pinchas asked his students how one recognizes the moment when night ends and day begins. "Is it the moment that it is light enough to tell a dog from a sheep?" one of the pupils asked. "No," the rabbi answered. "Is it the moment when we can tell a date palm from a fig tree?" the second asked. "No, that's not it, either," the rabbi replied. "So when does morning come, then?" the pupils asked. "It's the moment when we look into the face of any person and recognize them as our brother or sister," Rabbi Pinchas said. "Until we're able to do that, it's still night."[1]

It doesn't work to stand on a street corner and yell at people. Instead, truth is when we sit at the table, facing one another and breaking bread. God has made the table a holy place. We aren't left guessing what the kingdom of Jesus looks like when we can read what it looked like on earth. And one of the main components was Jesus *ate* with people. He sat down with them.

There is something mysterious and beautiful about the table. The table is scandalous and subversive.

While Jesus did a lot of eating with folks and proclaiming that the kingdom of heaven is near, we'd do right to follow suit. What if we invited those we disagreed with—or whose perspectives we are completely removed from—over for dinner?

HOW JESUS DOES BIBLE STUDY

In Scripture the table is closely linked with truth. It's the place of learning. The place of experience. The place of teaching. The people who care about truth should care about the table, because in Scripture you can't have one without the other. Only in our post-modern thinking have we put so much weight on mental assent and facts that would've been completely foreign to many cultures before us.

One of my favorite—and probably one of the most underrated—stories in all Scripture is after Jesus resurrects. He was just crucified by the Romans, and all hope that he was the one to restore Israel was crushed. I can only imagine the feeling of disappointment for some disciples who had followed Jesus for years, just to see him strung up on a piece of wood like a criminal. A crucified Messiah wasn't a Messiah to any person in the first century.

Then Sunday happens. The tomb opens, blood starts pumping in his veins, and the whole earth shakes. Human history takes a radical left turn at the resurrection of Jesus. God's answer to the world's problem is Jesus, and he won.

You'd think the first thing Jesus would do after such a cataclysmic event would be of epic proportions, but it's almost anticlimactic.

The gospel of Luke describes two guys who are

walking on the road to Emmaus, recounting all that transpired over the last few days. They were probably trying to process what had just happened. While they were talking, Jesus joined them, yet "their eyes were kept from recognizing him."

Jesus asks what they are talking about. They then almost sarcastically shoot back, "Are you the only visitor to Jerusalem who does not know the things that have happened there in these days?"

Where have you been, bro?

They even go on to admit they had high hopes for Jesus and "hoped that he was the one to redeem Israel." They believe that hope was crushed the minute Jesus died. Jesus' words then become very sharp to the two guys: "Foolish ones, and slow of heart to believe all that the prophets have spoken! Was it not necessary that the Christ should suffer these things and enter into his glory?"

Translation: Are you guys stupid? The Messiah was supposed to die the whole time! (Maybe he could've cut the guys some slack since up to that time almost no one in all history had read the Prophets expecting a crucified and strung-up Messiah. This reminds us that there are ways to read the Bible and completely miss Jesus.)

Jesus then "interpreted to them in all the Scriptures the things concerning himself."[2]

In Jesus' day, the complete Bible was what

Christians call the Old Testament or what modern Jews call the Hebrew Bible or *Tanakh*. So Jesus himself, God in flesh, explained the *entire* Old Testament to them. Jesus literally began on page 1, and walked them through to the end, and showed how he was the answer the whole time, without them knowing who he was.

The very Creator of the universe was the one explaining the Scriptures to these guys. They weren't left guessing anymore. God himself was saying, "Look! This should've happened the whole time. Let's start on page 1 and I'll show you all the way through."

You'd think their minds would have been absolutely blown away and they would have started seeing the matrix numbers running down the screen with scriptural truth, but nothing seems to happen.

They keep walking, and when they get close to Emmaus, they see Jesus is going farther, so they ask him to stay with them for the night. In Middle Eastern culture it was an honor to have someone stay with you, especially if they had farther to go and it was getting late.

The first thing they do is sit at a table and have a meal. But something crazy happens: "When he was at table with them, he took the bread and blessed and broke it and gave it to them. And their eyes were opened, and they recognized him."

Jesus walks through the entire Bible with these two guys and nothing happens. Then he rips a piece of bread in half, and they immediately recognize him.

They even go on to say after that, "Did not our hearts burn within us while he talked to us on the road?"[3]

This almost makes our Western minds short-circuit. The heart change, the opening of eyes, the revelation, the epiphany, whatever you want to call it—it didn't happen when they got all the facts; it happened when they sat at the table. It happened when they ate a meal. When there was relationship.

It's hard not to believe the table and a meal are important to Jesus and the Scriptures after hearing a story like that. But what's funny is that a lot of us would much rather have our eyes opened in the first scenario.

Our dream version of Christianity is having all the answers. Can't Jesus just show up in my room visibly and audibly tell me what to do and believe? News flash: he did to two guys, and it didn't help as much as we'd think.

Yet when they sat down with him, their lives changed.

Here's a hard question to ask ourselves: Would we rather have Jesus give us all the answers, or would we rather sit at the table with him?

Don't get me wrong. Truth is vital. The Scriptures

are my favorite thing to study, to listen to, to immerse myself in. But Jesus always, always, always couples truth with flesh. With intimacy. With real life.

Christianity isn't a college exam—we don't need to memorize and regurgitate facts. Jesus wants to open our eyes when we are sitting at the table building a relationship with him. One requires relationship; one doesn't. A sit-down meal is long, it's conversational, it's back and forth, and it's beautiful.

What if that was how we saw Christianity? No wonder Jesus himself uses language such as "wedding reception," "party," and "feast" to describe the kingdom of heaven.

Our dream version of following Jesus is to have all the facts. Jesus' dream of us following him is to sit with us.

Every morning when I open the Scriptures, part of me wants to just do it to check it off my list. I do it to get the answers for the day. But the days that are filled with hope, peace, and love are when I see that time in the morning as simply sitting with Jesus. Knowing him. Talking to him. Learning from him.

It's more of a discipline than anything. It requires so much effort for me just to sit there. To be silent and listen for a little bit, then talk to him and thank him for all he's done, and then to ask questions and ask for help. Prayer and Bible reading are a dialogue, not a monologue.

The problem is, we don't see how pervasive the problem is in our Western Christianity. In almost every aspect of our Christian lives, we are trained to take the life, flesh, and intimacy out and leave just a skeleton of facts.

Take Communion, for example. Most of us who have taken it, or seen it before, might differ on the specifics of how it should be done, but many of us still make it more abstract than it was originally meant to be.

The Last Supper was an actual feast. Jesus linked his death to a meal so that we'd never forget our need for it, since we have to eat all the time. He said, "Every time you break bread and drink wine, remember me."

And after the resurrection the early church restructured the tone of the meal to be celebratory in nature. It was a love feast. Communion in the early church was a table. It was a place where everyone was welcome. (The only time it's mentioned in Paul's letters, he condemned the Corinthians sharply for making it a country club where not everyone was welcome.)

It represented mutual love, sacrifice, and service. There they showed they were all equally in need of grace and forgiveness and would take the bread and wine together as signs pointing to Jesus and his death. It was a marker of Jesus followers.

A TABLE THAT HEALS

As someone who's dealt with serious seasons of lone-liness, brokenness, and even depression, I've found one place of incredible grace to be Psalm 78: "They spoke against God, saying, / 'Can God spread a table in the wilderness?'"[4]

Can God really prepare a table in the wilder-ness? To ancient Israel the wilderness represented death, ache, pain, and hurt. Nothing grew out there in the desert landscape. Like the Israelites in Psalm 78, I've found myself grumbling sarcastically or bit-terly saying the very same thing. They weren't asking earnestly but to show they thought God *couldn't* do it. But when we ask God a question, sometimes his answer can surprise us.

One of the weirdest verses in the Old Testament is in the book of Hosea. Israel is rebelling and not wor-shiping God. And to remedy that he says, "I will allure her, / and bring her into the wilderness, / and speak tenderly to her."[5]

There's this strange romance there. Where Israel saw dryness, a place no one wanted to go, and a place that only represented decay, God saw something different. *Allure* is such a tender word; it's as if God knows there are some things we can only learn in the wilderness.

It reminds me of the stars. If you think about it, the

stars are always out. In the daytime, if you look up, they are there. You just can't see them. It's only when it's dark that they shine, shimmer, and glow.

What if that's God? What if in the dark seasons, we looked up and saw his beauty? What if he glows brighter when we think everything is spinning out of control? Because if we are honest, we know that sometimes the best place to see the stars in all their glory is the wilderness.

And right in the middle of Israel's (and our) bitter or sarcastic questioning, God's answer is yes. He really does prepare a table in the wilderness. He prepares a table in the silence. He prepares a table in the depression. He prepares a table in the growing pains.

The God of the cosmos prepares a table for you and me. He meets with us and doesn't leave us out in the cold. He prepares a table right in the middle of racial tension in Ferguson, he prepares a table for Israelis and Palestinians, and he prepares a table for you and me. We are invited to sit, to eat, to learn, to laugh, and, most importantly, to love.

What a beautiful picture that God not only prepares a table for us, but he sits with us. He looks at us. God became man and dwelt among us. The Word bowed and pitched a tent in our midst. You don't have to go searching for God because he's right there smack-dab in the middle of any table where everyone is invited.

We are all in the family. We are diverse, we are unique, and we are all the very body of our King, Jesus. We share the same last name, and that's what matters. The saying goes that "blood is thicker than water," and that saying is true. But it isn't our blood that unites us but his. And what's best is, like a true family should, we are all invited to the table. The question is, will you have a seat?

The last time I was in Israel we were invited to a worship night. What I didn't know, though, was that it was an unadvertised secret worship night with some of the most influential Palestinian and Jewish Christians in the area. It had to be during a certain part of the year because that was the easiest for everyone to get through the border crossing and past the checkpoints.

At the top of their lungs grown men in both Arabic and Hebrew were shouting the praises of Jesus. I would have taken pictures or video, but it was strictly forbidden. Many people could've lost their jobs or even lives if others knew they were there with their supposed enemies. But it didn't matter I couldn't take pictures—I'll never forget it.

Hearing Yeshua (Jesus in Hebrew) and Isa (Jesus in Arabic) proclaimed in a room where most people had siblings or parents lost in the wars and intifadas was nothing short of amazing grace. Toward the end of the night, they began dancing. I got taken up front with some of the adult men, and we formed a circle with our arms over one another's shoulders and began dancing and singing.

I didn't understand one word they were saying except *Yeshua*, but I do know they were excited and couldn't contain their love for their brothers or for Jesus. I remember looking to my left and to my right and seeing a highly influential Palestinian man and then a highly influential Israeli man, both singing and dancing and locked arm in arm.

I believe this is what heaven will look like. It's no wonder in Revelation the end of time is described as a "marriage supper of the Lamb."[6]

In one of John's visions he sees *all* tribes, and *all* people, and *all* languages standing before the throne crying out with a loud voice, "Salvation belongs to our God who sits on the throne, and to the Lamb!"[7]

That's our end goal. We already know the end of the story, but here's the question: Is the trajectory of our life putting us there? Or are we on a different path?

The reason table and intimacy and story and temple and Sabbath are so important is that they are relational. You can't tell a story unless you have a relationship with your listeners. You can't have intimacy without another person. You can't enjoy the power of the table unless other people are there.

And what would our lives look like if we returned

to that? So many young people are "leaving the faith" after they get older because they never really knew the faith in the first place. Or a better way to say it is maybe they never really knew Jesus.

It's easy to leave facts. It's easy to change your mind. It's easy to throw something off and forget it.

But it's awfully hard to forget a person. To forget a relationship. To miss out on being known and loved and forgiven at the same time. That's what Jesus is offering and that's what we are invited to.

To sit at the table with him.

He invited us long ago. It's about time we take a seat.

NOTES

Chapter 1: Creation: Our Place in God's Story

1. Genesis 1:26–27.
2. I first saw this distinction in Jonathan Martin, *Prototype: What Happens When You Discover You're More Like Jesus Than You Think?* (Chicago: Tyndale, 2013).
3. Genesis 1:27, emphasis added.
4. Dallas Willard, *The Divine Conspiracy* (New York: HarperCollins, 1998).
5. David Franzoni, *Amistad*, directed by Steven Spielberg (1997; Universal City: Dreamworks Video, 1999), DVD.
6. N. T. Wright, *Surprised by Scripture* (San Francisco: HarperOne, 2014), 138.
7. Wright, *Surprised by Scripture*, 135.
8. God can and does use every means to draw us to himself. He is bigger than our ways but surely can use our frail, feeble, and sometimes distorted attempts to

share his gospel. But his ability and willingness to use
our failures for his kingdom shouldn't keep us from
pursuing the best option and telling the better story.

Chapter 2: Incarnation: God's Tent in Our Backyard

1. Exodus 29:45.
2. Revelation 21:3.
3. Exodus 25:8; Leviticus 26:12; Zechariah 2:10;
   2 Corinthians 6:16; Revelation 21:3.
4. 1 Kings 6:1; 1 Chronicles 22.
5. Jeremiah 52.
6. Psalm 137:1–3.

Chapter 3: Intimacy: Living with God

1. Genesis 3:7–8.
2. Genesis 3:11.
3. C. S. Lewis, *The Four Loves* (New York: Harcourt,
   1960), 121.

Chapter 4: Identity: Understanding Who You Are

1. N. T. Wright, *Surprised by Hope* (San Francisco:
   HarperOne, 2008), 29.
2. Luke 3:22.
3. Jonathan Martin, *Prototype: What Happens When
   You Discover You're More Like Jesus Than You Think?*
   (Chicago: Tyndale, 2013), 18.
4. Luke 15:15–16.
5. Matthew 3:17.

NOTES

Chapter 5: Sabbath: The Blessing of Rest

1. John Ortberg, *Soul Keeping* (Grand Rapids: Zondervan, 2014), 126.
2. Thanks to Curtis Yates for posing this exact question to me in the process of writing this book.
3. Abraham Joshua Heschel, *The Sabbath* (New York: Farrar, Straus and Giroux, 2005).
4. Abraham Joshua Heschel, *God in Search of Man* (New York: Farrar, Straus and Giroux, 1976), 417.

Chapter 6: Worship: Reflecting God's Glory

1. C. S. Lewis, *The Great Divorce* (1945; repr., San Francisco: HarperOne, 2009), 39.
2. Psalm 115:4–5.
3. Revelation 5:13.

Chapter 7: God's Kingdom: Heaven on Earth

1. I've read this idea multiple places but especially remember Michael Hidalgo's book *Unlost* (Downers Grove, IL: InterVarsity Press, 2014), where he notes Caesar had many titles that Jesus claimed for himself.
2. John 13:4–5.
3. John 13:16.
4. N. T. Wright, *Simply Jesus: A New Vision of Who He Was, What He Did, and Why He Matters* (New York: HarperCollins, 2011), 218.
5. Luke 19:42.
6. Matthew 5:43–45.

7. Brian Zahnd, *Beauty Will Save the World* (Lake Mary, FL: Charisma House, 2012), 217.

8. Colossians 3:17.

9. 1 Timothy 4:4–5.

10. 1 Thessalonians 5:18.

Chapter 8: Brokenness: Taking Off the Mask

1. Thanks to John Mark Comer and his book *Loveology* (Grand Rapids, MI: Zondervan, 2014), where I first heard the difference between scars and wounds.

2. Zephaniah 3:17.

3. 1 Corinthians 6:18.

4. John 20:25.

5. John 20:27.

Chapter 9: Fellowship: The Power of the Table

1. Tomáš Halík, *Night of the Confessor: Christian Faith in an Age of Uncertainty* (New York: Doubleday Religion, 2012), 176.

2. Luke 24:13–27.

3. Luke 24:30–32.

4. Psalm 78:19.

5. Hosea 2:14.

6. Revelation 19:9.

7. Revelation 7:9–10.

ABOUT THE AUTHOR

Jefferson Bethke is the *New York Times* bestselling author of *Jesus > Religion* and *It's Not What You Think*. He and his wife, Alyssa, host *The Real Life Podcast* each week and make YouTube videos that are watched by hundreds of thousands of viewers each month. They also cofounded *Family Teams*, an online initiative that helps families live out God's design by equipping and encouraging them to build a multi-generational team on mission (in all of its different expressions). They live in Maui with their daughter, Kinsley; son, Kannon; new baby girl, Lucy; and dog, Aslan. To say hi or to learn more, go to http://jeffandalyssa.com.